What Does the Bible Say About the End Times?
A Catholic View

FR. WILLIAM KURZ, S.J.

SERVANT
BOOKS

PUBLISHED BY ST. ANTHONY MESSENGER PRESS
CINCINNATI, OHIO

Nihil Obstat: Hilarion Kistner, OFM
          Reverend Timothy P. Schehr

Imprimi Potest: Fred Link, OFM
          Reverend John M. Paul, S.J.

Imprimatur: †Most Reverend Carl K. Moeddel, Vicar General and
          Auxiliary Bishop
          Archdiocese of Cincinnati, July 19, 2004

The *nihil obstat* and *imprimatur* are a declaration that a book or pamphlet is considered to be free from doctrinal or moral error. It is not implied that those who have granted the *nihil obstat* and *imprimatur* agree with the contents, opinions or statements expressed.

Unless otherwise noted, Scripture passages have been taken from the *Revised Standard Version*, Catholic edition. Copyright 1946, 1952, 1971 by the Division of Christian Education of the National Council of Churches of Christ in the U.S.A. Used by permission. All rights reserved.

Cover design by Candle Light Studios
Book design by Emily Schneider

Library of Congress Cataloging-in-Publication Data

Kurz, William S., 1939-
    What does the Bible say about the end times? : a Catholic view /
William
Kurz.
        p. cm.
    Includes index.
    ISBN 0-86716-606-1 (alk. paper)
  1. Rapture (Christian eschatology) 2. Eschatology—Biblical
teaching. 3.
Catholic Church—Doctrines. I. Title.

BT887.K87 2004
236—dc22

                    2004015672

ISBN 0-86716-606-1

Servant Books is an imprint of St. Anthony Messenger Press.
Published by St. Anthony Messenger Press
www.AmericanCatholic.org
Printed in the United States of America

To Fr. William Dooley, S.J.

TABLE OF CONTENTS

Acknowledgments

This book presupposes two fine explicit recent Catholic apologetic responses to contemporary theories of the rapture: Paul Thigpen, *The Rapture Trap: A Catholic Response to "End Times" Fever* (West Chester, Penn.: Ascension, 2001) and Carl E. Olson, *Will Catholics Be "Left Behind"? A Catholic Critique of the Rapture and Today's Prophecy Preachers* (San Francisco: Ignatius, 2003). This book's primary focus will not be apologetic responses to such theories but a personal consultation as a Catholic Scripture scholar of what the Bible reveals about the end times. I am especially grateful to Paul Thigpen, who persuaded me of the need for a book like this.

I also want to mention in gratitude three people who have helped me in the research, writing, and editing of this book. I am particularly grateful to Fr. William Dooley, S.J., to whom I dedicate this book. His editorial assistance on chapters one through four was invaluable. Unfortunately he died before I could get him my fifth chapter. May he rest in peace.

I am also very grateful to my teaching assistant, Jeremy Holmes, and to Dr. Patrick Doyle, both of Marquette University, for their extensive bibliographical and editorial help over several months.

Introduction

For decades Evangelical Protestants have confronted Catholics with the question "Are you saved?" More recently Catholics find themselves also contending with the at least implied question "Will you be left behind?" Such questions and widespread end time speculations lend urgency to the question about what sense Catholics are to make of the end times predictions and passages in the Bible.

Rapture, antichrist, tribulation, and judgment scenarios fascinate many Christians (sometimes to the point of obsession). Relatively few Catholics are among these, although rumors of "secrets" and predictions of disasters in reports of Marian apparitions have aroused similar anxieties among some.[1]

Nevertheless, biblical questions about the end of the world, or even about the end of history as we know it, are quite serious and demand the attention of all Christians, including Catholics. Furthermore, the apocalyptic biblical texts that treat these matters can be rather confusing, even for trained exegetes, whose forte is the critical interpretation and explanation of Scripture. In fact, early church fathers (from the second century to St. Augustine to St. Thomas Aquinas and beyond) grappled with the same apocalyptic passages and asked many of the same questions as Protestants today. Texts like the Book of Revelation leave themselves open to many interpretations and explanations, so that among those early writers also there were many disagreements and differences.

Some of the current differences of theological emphases that separate Catholics (and Orthodox) from fundamentalist Protestants help explain the different levels of interest in possible end time scenarios. End times enthusiasts tend to emphasize Christ's current absence from earth and his dwelling place in heaven, whence he shall return. Of course, Catholicism also believes in Christ's ascension and consequent physical absence from earth, and the hope of his return is a central biblical doctrine that cannot be overlooked. But in comparison to many of those Protestants who are fascinated by end times discussions, Catholics tend to have a stronger sense that the risen Christ is present now among us—with his Church and in the sacraments.[2]

Biblical scholarship has pointed out a pattern in Scripture that helps provide a context in which to understand the emphasis in the Bible on the end times (technically referred to as eschatology) and on revelations of the mysteries of the End (technically referred to as apocalypses). A German expression for this pattern is that the Endzeit (end time) is portrayed by analogy to the Urzeit (time of the beginning); that is, the final or eschatological times are portrayed by analogy to the primeval creation of the world.[3]

Because of this tendency among writers of apocalypses, readers need to be sensitized to the many echoes in apocalyptic texts such as Revelation to the Creation and Fall accounts in Genesis, especially in the so-called "primeval history" in Genesis 1–11 leading up to the story of Abraham. Particularly rich sources of the imagery in Revelation are the first three chapters of Genesis, which recount the creation of the world and of the human race, followed by the human rebellion and fall. For example, the vision of God's final victory in Revelation 20–21 recalls the Tree of Life in Eden: A new creation replaces the old; the Lord and the Lamb replace the sun and the moon; the river from the throne brings to mind the four rivers around Eden. Likewise, the fertile trees with fruit every month and with leaves for healing remind one of the trees of Eden.

Another important pattern, which is related to the Urzeit-Endzeit comparisons, is found in Orthodox and

Catholic liturgies and has been noted by scholars.[4] It is the centrality of the temple and (Mount) Zion and (the New) Jerusalem in apocalyptic writing in general and in Revelation in particular. Revelation portrays the heavens opening in a setting that has associations with the temple and Mount Zion (even though the seer John is situated on the island of Patmos).

Orthodox and Catholic liturgies have consistently emphasized the presence of the risen Christ by using many of the symbols and paraphernalia of the temple and ancient priesthood. In the Eucharist we join the angelic hosts in worshipping God: "Holy, Holy, Holy, Lord God of hosts. Heaven and earth are full of your glory. Hosanna in the highest. Blessed is he who comes in the name of the Lord. Hosanna in the highest."

Mount Zion and the temple become the meeting place between earth and heaven, humans and God, throughout much of the Old Testament as well as the New Testament, including Revelation. Several of the details mentioned in Revelation relate to the temple, such as the seven candlesticks (the Jewish menorah). Others relate to the priesthood: The seal on the foreheads of the saints in Revelation 7:3 reminds us of the engraved plate Aaron wore on his, bearing the words "Holy to the Lord."[5] In Revelation the primary image for Jesus is the Lamb who was slain, which alludes to the temple sacrifices of lambs both at Passover and throughout the year.

Many visions of the end times vividly portray judgment on all sin (from the "original sin" in Genesis 3 on) and restoration of the divinely intended order that was destroyed by sin. This restoration often takes the form of a "new creation" and involves a "son of man" who will function as a new Adam, undoing the damage from the original man. For example, the serpent of Genesis 3 returns as the dragon of Revelation 12, and the son of the woman overcomes the dragon. This victory will repair the disorder wrought by the serpent's successful temptation of the first woman and Adam. The new creation will again allow access to the Tree of Life, from which humans were barred after the Fall by the angel with flaming sword. The new creation will have neither sea nor darkness, which are elements of chaos relating to the first creation. It will need no sun nor moon, for it will be illuminated by the glory of the Lord and of the Lamb.

To understand the often puzzling solutions and answers in the Book of Revelation, it is important to know the problems and questions that they try to address. In view of the way the Bible tends to explain the end times in terms of the "beginning," a good introduction to these problems can be found by analyzing Genesis 1–3. These chapters lay the narrative foundation in creation for the "primeval history" in Genesis 1–11, which in turn introduce the account about God's saving work through the patriarchs in the rest of Genesis, beginning with the call of Abraham in Genesis 12.

A predominant concern in apocalyptic literature about the end times is to find a solution to the problem of evil. Why does evil seem so dominant in our world, often to the detriment of good people and believers? Where is the justice in this world, where evil people can get away with wickedness and the good suffer unfairly? How can there be an all-just and all-powerful God when so much evil seems not only to exist but even to flourish and dominate human history?

Even many of the more grotesque depictions of God's wrath and horrible punishments in apocalyptic writings become more understandable when viewed as a response to the problem of evil. The biblical response to this problem finds its foundation and starting point in the account of the Creation and Fall in Genesis 1–3. Our first step in reflecting on the end times and their judgments will be to consider the "beginning" and the first sin, which necessitates such judgments.

Notes:

1. Ralph Martin, *Is Jesus Coming Soon? A Catholic Perspective on the Second Coming* (San Francisco: Ignatius, 1983), 135-36.

2. Carl E. Olson, *Will Catholics Be "Left Behind"? A Catholic Critique of the Rapture and Today's Prophecy Preachers* (San Francisco: Ignatius, 2003), 348-49.

3. See Brevard S. Childs, *Myth and Reality in the Old Testament* (Studies in Biblical Theology, 27; 2nd ed.; London: SCM, 1962), 77-84.

4. See Jon D. Levenson, *Sinai and Zion: An Entry into the Jewish Bible* (New York: Harper SanFrancisco, 1985); Scott Hahn, *The Lamb's Supper: The Mass as Heaven on Earth* (New York: Doubleday, 1999); Margaret Barker, *On Earth as It Is in Heaven: Temple Symbolism in the New Testament* (Edinburgh: T&T Clark, 1995). For more thorough treatments see Pilchan Lee, *The New Jerusalem in the Book of Revelation: A Study of Revelation 21-22 in the Light of Its Background in Jewish Tradition* (Wissenschaftliche Untersuchungen zum Neuen Testament, 2nd series, 129; Tübingen, Germany: Mohr Siebeck, 2001); Gregory Stevenson, *Power and Place: Temple and Identity in the Book of Revelation* (Beihefte zur Zeitschrift für die neutestamentliche Wissenschaft und die Kunde der älteren Kirche, 107; New York: Walter de Gruyter, 2001).

5. Compare Exodus 28:36-38; Revelation 7:3 and 22:4. Contrast the mark of the beast and the harlot in Revelation 13:16; 17:5.

chapter one

In the Beginning: Genesis 1–3

Where did we come from? Where are we going? These two questions locate our human race in this world and in relationship to God. The Bible addresses the question about our origins at the beginning of Genesis, its first book. The question about our destiny finds its classic biblical response in the last book of the Christian Bible, Revelation. In treating the question about our destination, this last book relies heavily on the Genesis treatment of whence we have come.

Many of Revelation's visions for the end times reintroduce God's plan in creating the universe and the primeval conditions "in the beginning," before the Fall. Revelation correspondingly emphasizes a "new creation," which restores what was spoiled in God's original plan for a good creation in Genesis. But Revelation also has to account for human insurrection and withdrawal from God's friendship and for the horrible evils that have resulted from them.

To answer our original questions concisely, we come from God our Creator, and we are to return to God our Judge. St. Augustine emphasized one positive aspect of this: "You have made us for yourself, O God, and our hearts are restless until they rest in you."[1]

Creator God

Scripture begins quite simply, "In the beginning." As interpreted by Christians today, this statement differs sharply from the widespread presumption in the ancient world that the "stuff" from which the world was shaped always existed. Greek philosophers later came to refer to this belief as "the eternity of matter."[2] Many historical critics argue that Genesis likewise simply presupposes some preexisting chaos onto which God imposes order (the Greek word for order is *cosmos*).

However, as Luke Johnson and I argued in our *Future of Catholic Biblical Scholarship*, the biblical worldview as read by Catholics has evolved well beyond whatever perspectives the original writers of this creation account may have had.[3] Most historical critics examine Genesis in relationship to its ancient Near Eastern environment, to stages in its composition, and to its original historical setting. Although this procedure produces many valuable insights, it also has the negative result of alienating the text from contemporary concerns and beliefs and of providing it a context thousands of years in the past.

Although establishing original meanings of Scripture remains essential, a contemporary Catholic reading has to look at Genesis from the perspective of its place in the canonical Christian Scriptures (including the New Testament) and within the traditional and current faith of the Church. The approach of this book will, from the perspective of a biblical exegete, presuppose the historical reconstruction of original meaning. But it will emphasize the Bible's canonical meanings and its message for Catholic believers today.

At least in the context of the overall scriptural canon and as commonly interpreted by later Jewish and Christian biblical writers, Genesis provides a different perspective from those of its pagan predecessors. The heavens and earth come exclusively from God, who "created" them. The Hebrew uses *bara*, "created," not the ordinary word for "to make" that describes God's making of the firmament (Genesis 1:7) or of the sun and moon in the heavens (1:16). Genesis uses this special word in Hebrew for the original creation of heavens and earth (Genesis 1:1), for the creation of living beings (1:21), repeatedly for the creation of humans (1:27), and to summarize all God's work of creation in Genesis 2:3.

Wisdom and Word

Not only the early chapters of Genesis but much of the Old Testament emphasize that God is the Creator of the world as we know it. As merely one example, later chapters of Isaiah (chapters 40–55, which are often referred to as "Second Isaiah") repeatedly insist that God created everything, including humans.[5] As Israelites continued to reflect on their belief in God's creation (as this belief can now be found in Genesis), they stressed that God created everything by his wisdom and by his word.

Both the psalmist and the author of Proverbs specify that God did his work of creation by divine wisdom: "O LORD, how manifold are thy works! In wisdom hast thou made them all; the earth is full of thy creatures" (Psalm 104:24). "The LORD by wisdom founded the earth; by understanding he established the heavens" (Proverbs 3:19). The prophet Jeremiah also attributes creation to God's wisdom: "It is he who made the earth by his power, who established the world by his wisdom, and by his understanding stretched out the heavens" (Jeremiah 10:12 [and 51:15]).

When later Old and New Testament writers reflected on the creation account in which God said repeatedly, "Let there be…" followed by the immediate result "and it was so," they came to the reasonable conclusion that God's creation was by his Word alone. Creation was not achieved by some mythic battle over chaos or monsters, even though such mythic symbols and images remain in poetic passages throughout the Old Testament and will return in the symbolism of the Book of Revelation. The psalmist expressed it thus: "By the word of the LORD the heavens were made, and all their host by the breath of his mouth" (Psalm 33:6). This particular verse will even come to have Trinitarian implications later, when Christians meditate on it, since it contains the words "Lord," "Word," and "breath" ("Spirit" in Hebrew, Greek, and Latin).

In the Book of Wisdom (written after 30 B.C.),[6] "Solomon" begins his prayer by reprising Genesis 1: "O God of my fathers and Lord of mercy, who hast made all things by thy word, and by thy wisdom hast formed man, to have dominion over the creatures thou hast made" (Wisdom 9:1-2). The New Testament Book of Revelation at least implies that God's creation is by his Word alone in its song of the twenty-four elders in Revelation 4:11: "Worthy art thou, our Lord and God, to receive glory and honor and power, for thou didst create all things, and by thy will they existed and were created." (The Greek text of the New Testament does not use *made* here, as the Septuagint does in chapter one of Genesis, but *created*.)

Around A.D. 100 the Jewish author of the non-canonical 4 Ezra refers repeatedly to the Genesis creation account and to God's creating by his word alone.[7] In 4 Ezra 6:38, the seer ("Ezra") remarks, "O Lord, thou didst speak at the beginning of creation, and didst say on the first day, Let heaven and earth be made, and thy word accomplished the work." Elsewhere the seer gives the reason behind the Lord's knowing the inner thoughts of humans: "[God] said, 'Let the earth be made,' and it was made; 'Let the heaven be made,' and it was made. At his word the stars were fixed, and he knows the number of the stars" (4 Ezra 16:55-56). When discussing the need for God's mercy, the seer refers to "those who were created by his word" (4 Ezra 7:69).

Creatio ex Nihilo

The progression from belief in creation by God's word alone to belief in creation "from nothing" (*ex nihilo*) is a logical and easy one. The earliest distinct biblical intimation about creation "from nothing" occurs in the plea of the Maccabean mother of seven sons in 2 Maccabees 7:28: "I beseech you, my child, to look at the heaven and the earth and see everything that is in them, and recognize that God did not make them out of things that existed. Thus also mankind comes into being." Belief that God created everything out of nothing confirms the belief, now urgently needed by the Maccabeans, that God can raise them from the dead if they allow themselves to be martyred for their faith.[8]

In the New Testament the author of Hebrews combines an explicit claim that God created by his word (*rhema*, rather than the *logos* in John 1), with at least an implicit reference to creation from nothing: "By faith we understand that the world was created by the word of God, so that what is seen was made out of things which do not appear" (Hebrews 11:3). The Greek original refers to creating what is visible from "what is invisible," words that could imply "from nothing."

These reflections on the implications of the biblical accounts of God's creating simply by his word reflect an ancient belief in the power of the spoken word to perform what it says. Once a word is spoken it cannot be recalled, but its effect follows inevitably. Thus when Isaac is tricked into blessing Jacob instead of Esau, his blessing cannot be recalled, even though it was obtained through trickery (see Genesis 27:27-41). Note especially verse 33, "I have blessed him?—yes, and he shall be blessed," and verse 35, "But [Isaac] said, 'Your brother came with guile, and he has taken away your blessing.'" As powerful as this conception of the spoken word was, both Jewish and Christian interpreters took the further step of personifying the word, sometimes as Wisdom, sometimes as Word.[9]

John 1's Interpretation
Christian readers find an authoritative interpretation of Genesis 1 in the prologue of the Gospel of John. When the author begins his account by deliberately echoing the

beginning of Genesis, he is building on centuries of Jewish reflection (often described as *midrashic*) on the implications of close and prayerful reading of the Creation account. When John recounts how God created by his word alone, his interpretation refers explicitly to Jesus (that is, it is a christological interpretation). He identifies the Word as God's Son: "In the beginning was the Word, and the Word was with God, and the Word was God. He was in the beginning with God; all things were made through him, and without him was not anything made that was made.... We have beheld his glory, glory as of the only Son from the Father" (John 1:1-3 and 14b).

The step from a statement like "By the word of the LORD the heavens were made" (Psalm 33:6) to "All things were made through him" [that is, through the Word of God] requires personifying *word* as "the Word." Most scholars find intermediate precedents for this kind of personification in the Old Testament personification of wisdom. That personification was stimulated by Jewish reflection on biblical references to God's creating by his wisdom.

Thus Proverbs refers to God's creating wisdom before the rest of creation. It relates how Wisdom consequently was present as a "master workman" (Proverbs 8:30) beside God during the rest of creation (Proverbs 8:22-30).[10] The later Book of Wisdom (about 30 B.C.), in a passage extolling Wisdom's virtues (Wisdom 7:22–8:1), refers to Wisdom as "the fashioner of all things" (7:22). The Book of Wisdom understands Wisdom not only as participating in creation but also as guiding salvation history in a way that patristic authors such as Justin Martyr would later apply to the pre-incarnate Word (Wisdom 10–12).

The Saving Word
Like Genesis, John's Gospel goes back to "the beginning." John interprets "In the beginning God created the heavens

and the earth" (Genesis 1:1) in the light of Genesis 1:3, "And God said, 'Let there be light'; and there was light" (see similar statements in Genesis 1:6, 9, 11, 14-15, 24). In Genesis, when God says, "Let there be...," the response is always "And it was so." Thus John concludes that the Word through which God created everything was with God "in the beginning." To preserve the unity of God, John makes clear that this Word who was with God "was God" (John 1:1): "He was in the beginning with God; all things were made through him, and without him was not anything made that was made" (1:2-3).

John's Gospel reflects on Genesis 1–2 in the light of Genesis 3–11, of the entire Old Testament history of sin and salvation, and of the saving event of Christ. Therefore it emphasizes the role of God's Word not merely in creation but also in salvation (or re-creation or the "new creation"). After sin infiltrated the world, the Word through whom God created the world also entered that created world, but he was not generally recognized or received by the world or even by his own people.

> The true light that enlightens every man was coming into the world. He was in the world, and the world was made through him, yet the world knew him not. He came to his own home, and his own people received him not.
>
> JOHN 1:9-11

The quite unforeseeably generous way that the Word entered the world was by actually becoming a man: "And the Word became flesh and dwelt among us, full of grace and truth; we have beheld his glory, glory as of the only Son from the Father" (1:14). The God who created humans and who was offended by human rebellion actually took on human nature himself "and dwelt among us."

The Spiritual Exercises

There is a Latin maxim, the truth of which is commonly conceded, even by skeptical scholars, *Lex orandi, lex credendi:* "The way in which people pray is a good indication of what they believe." Therefore, in addition to applying my biblical expertise to the task of interpreting Scripture, this book will also consider how Catholic Christians have prayed over Scripture. The cardinal example of Christian prayer is the liturgy, especially the Eucharist. But there are also some especially powerful meditations of St. Ignatius Loyola on Creation, Incarnation, and the situation of the human as creature before God as Creator and in relation to the rest of created beings. They are found in St. Ignatius' *Spiritual Exercises*, which have been especially recommended by the Church to systematize spiritual retreats for Jesuits, other priests, religious, and lay people.

The *Spiritual Exercises* contain profound meditations and contemplations that articulate their vision of the world and of human history. Evidently grounded in the Genesis creation accounts, the bedrock for the Ignatian vision is "The First Principle and Foundation":

> Man is created to praise, reverence, and serve God our Lord, and by this means to save his soul. The other things on the face of the earth are created for man to help him in attaining the end for which he is created. Hence, man is to make use of them in as far as they help him in the attainment of his end, and he must rid himself of them in as far as they prove a hindrance to him.[11]

The relationship of this Ignatian principle to Genesis 1–2 becomes apparent when we simply recall the main statements in the combined Genesis creation accounts: In the beginning God created the heavens and the earth and eventually created man, male and female, in his image and likeness. God placed humans over the rest of material creation, a dominion symbolized by their "tending the Garden of Eden." Humans also lived in intimate friendship with God their Creator. Then sin ruined God's original plan for creation and for the human race (Genesis 3–11).

At this point the *Spiritual Exercises* ponder how the Trinitarian God himself comes to our rescue, as powerfully visualized in the contemplation on the Incarnation. That contemplation envisions the Trinity, who created the world and the human race, now observing human creatures filling the earth with sin and stampeding headlong toward hell. In compassion the Trinity determines that the Second Person, the Son, will become incarnate to intervene and to save us from certain damnation. There are significant resonances between this Ignatian contemplation and the Old Testament accounts of human sins and God's saving actions, when they are interpreted through the prologue of John, as it likewise comments on the Old Testament accounts of the Creation and Fall.

John 1:4-5 clarifies the life-giving and revelatory nature of the Word and how this revealing light shines into the darkness created by human sin: "In him was life, and the life was the light of men. The light shines in the darkness, and the darkness has not overcome it." When the Word comes into the world, the world does not acknowledge him, and his own people to whom he comes do not accept him (see John 1:10-11). Nevertheless, there is no stopping the mission of the Word. Thus had Isaiah compared the Word of God to the rain that comes down from heaven and does not return without watering the earth: "So shall my word be that goes forth from my mouth; it shall not return to me empty, but it shall accomplish that which I purpose, and prosper in the thing for which I sent it" (Isaiah 55:11).

Despite the limited positive reception of God's Word (John 1:12-13), God did not abandon human sinners to their fate. Rather, in a most astounding manner, the divine

Word became one of us and shared our lot: "And the Word became flesh and dwelt among us, full of grace and truth" (John 1:14). As Genesis 1:26 portrays God in council with himself about making man in his image, so the Ignatian contemplation on the Incarnation imagines a dialogue within the Trinity that expresses the divine compassion for fallen humans, which motivates this astonishing action on God's part: that of condescending to become flesh and to dwell among us and share in our tragic plight.

John's Gospel goes on to identify this Word with the only Son of God (see John 1:14b) who also acts as "the Lamb of God, who takes away the sin of the world" (1:29). The Johannine *midrashic* reflection on the Creation and Fall in Genesis goes far beyond the primeval "beginning" to the subsequent conflict against evil and consequent suffering of God's incarnate Son and Word, which takes us beyond our present reflection on Genesis. However, John's prologue and Gospel provide a context and rationale for God's creative and saving activities in Genesis and beyond.

The warfare between good and evil that swirls around God's incarnate Word throughout most of John's Gospel provides direct canonical preparation and biblical justification for the final reckoning that the Book of Revelation will portray. The *Spiritual Exercises* also contribute supporting images about how the Son, Jesus, goes about doing this work of salvation and eliciting human followers to help in the task. A particularly fruitful meditation is the "Two Standards," where Satan and Christ are rallying their opposing forces of evil and good for the struggle to prevail over the world and its human inhabitants, again for evil or for good.[12] Both the fourth evangelist and Ignatius provide an overview perspective on the battles between God and Satan, good and evil, which in turn provide canonical underpinning for the opening of Revelation, in which John the seer is an exile on Patmos because of evil forces.

The New Creation

The Catholic interpretation of creation in Genesis therefore clearly asserts that God created everything by his word alone, without working on any preexisting matter. This makes God's creating action unique—clearly distinct from making one finished entity out of some material that existed previously, the only kind of making of which creatures are capable. The New Testament perceives this creative power of God as also active in the resurrection of Jesus, which it interprets as a "new creation" in which Christians can share: "Therefore, if any one is in Christ, he is a new creation; the old has passed away, behold, the new has come" (2 Corinthians 5:17); "But far be it from me to glory except in the cross of our Lord Jesus Christ, by which the world has been crucified to me, and I to the world. For neither circumcision counts for anything, nor uncircumcision, but a new creation" (Galatians 6:14-15).

In this manner St. Paul relates the unique original creative power of God to God's raising from the dead, a resurrection first manifested in God's raising Jesus and then promised by extension to all. Thus to the Corinthians Paul explains that suffering forced him to rely not on himself "but on God who raises the dead" (2 Corinthians 1:9). Colossians refers to "faith in the working of God, who raised [Jesus] from the dead" (Colossians 2:12b). In the New Testament, Christian faith in God's unique power as Creator was exemplified by and applied to the "new creation" of the resurrection of Jesus and to the future resurrection of Christians.

The Crown of Creation

The Genesis creation account followed its initial general statement, "In the beginning God created the heavens and the earth," with accounts of God's creation and ordering of the various elements of the world or cosmos. The climax of this creative activity came on "the sixth day." After God had made living creatures to inhabit the earth, he turned to the creation of man as the highest species on earth. The account hints at how special a creature man was to be by reporting that God took counsel before making man.

> Then God said, "Let us make man in our image, after our likeness; and let them have dominion over the fish of the sea, and over the birds of the air, and over the cattle, and over all the earth, and over every creeping thing that creeps upon the earth."
>
> GENESIS 1:26

After establishing God's unique power and authority as Creator of everything that is, Genesis situates humans as part of God's creation but as creation's crown, having authority over other material creatures. Psalm 8 responds with awe to man's exalted position among material creatures:

> When I look at thy heavens, the work of thy fingers,
>   the moon and the stars which thou hast established;
> what is man that thou art mindful of him,
>   and the son of man that thou dost care for him?
> Yet thou hast made him little less than God,
>   and dost crown him with glory and honor.
> Thou hast given him dominion over the works of thy hands;
>   thou hast put all things under his feet.
>
> PSALM 8:3-6[13]

The Image and Likeness of God

What is extraordinary about the creature man is that only he is in God's image. Ancient kings were often said to be the image of God, and that expression implied kingly authority over others. The Hebrew term for *image*, perhaps surprisingly to us, was also a common term for idols that humans were not to worship in place of the true God. (Thus the ten occurrences of image in Revelation 13–20 all refer to the idolatrous image of the beast.) From the Greek translation of image comes our English word *icon*, which is often applied to Jesus as icon of God.

That Adam was said to be created "in the image of God" implies Adam's kingly authority over the rest of material creation. Thus when Christians reflected on Christ as the New Adam, they applied the expression *image of God* to him in a preeminent way. Colossians 1:15, for example, says, "He is the image [icon in Greek] of the invisible God, the first-born of all creation." And 1 Corinthians 15:49 states, "Just as we have borne the image of the man of dust, we shall also bear the image of the man of heaven."

Although in Genesis 1:26 God said, "Let us make man in our image, after our likeness," the following verse 27 no longer mentions God's *likeness*: "So God created man in his own image, in the image of God he created him; male and female he created them." In the Greek Septuagint and New Testament, the word for *likeness* occurs nine times, but only the following instances seem relevant to our text: The condemnation of the king of Tyre by Ezekiel uses a rather vague expression: "Son of man, raise a lamentation over the king of Tyre, and say to him, Thus says the Lord GOD: 'You were the signet of perfection [literally "seal of likeness"]'" (Septuagint Greek of Ezekiel 28:12). This text appears to contain an allusion to the notion of *likeness* in Genesis 1:26, if it is describing the exalted king as a "seal of the likeness" [of God]. (In the Vulgate, the Latin word for *likeness* occurs most often in Ezekiel's visions, as an indirect way of describing God without drawing even a verbal image of God, since to do so would be perceived as violating the first commandment's prohibition of images of God.)

One Greek translation of Daniel uses the word *likeness* to compare angels to humans: "And behold, one in the likeness of the sons of men touched my lips" (Daniel 10:16).

The clearest allusion occurs in James 3:9: "With [our

tongue] we bless the Lord and Father, and with it we curse men, who are made in the likeness of God."

The biblical emphasis on man in God's image and its correlative silence (apart from James 3:9) about man in God's likeness are noteworthy and have drawn attention from patristic times to today. Some patristic writers have remarked how the image is freely given to us but the likeness must be attained.[14] Another theory to explain this silence is that even after their fall, humans continue to exist in God's image, but they no longer are in God's likeness. Both speculations furnish obvious motivations for homilies: namely, that we should strive for perfection in order that we may either obtain God's likeness or restore that lost likeness in ourselves.

Original Man

Christian reflection also finds significant implications in the statement that the image in which God created man was "male and female" (Genesis 1:27). *The Catechism of the Catholic Church* focuses on the dignity of a person who has self-awareness and can freely give himself in communion to others, an idea that is implied in the mention of man's being "male and female" (*CCC,* #357).[15] As God has revealed himself to be a communion of persons in the Trinity, man in God's image as male and female is also meant to be a communion of persons.

This communion is to find fruit in the blessing that God immediately gives them: "Be fruitful and multiply, and fill the earth and subdue it" (Genesis 1:28), an effect related to their dominion over all living creatures on the earth. Both the Hebrew and Greek words for *subdue* imply strong domination and control, with even some harsh overtones. In other words, the authority God gives his image is a comprehensive jurisdiction.

Nevertheless, that authority is delegated to man as the

image of God and acting as God's viceroy. As Psalm 8 put it, "Thou hast made him little less than God" (Psalm 8:5). This authority remains limited by God's higher authority and is to be exercised for the purposes that God intends. It is this limitation that will provide the psychological opening for the temptation, in Genesis 3, for humans to disregard God's commands and to become autonomous in their exercise of authority. No matter how exalted among creatures they are, humans will want to be not merely "little less than God" but "like God, knowing good and evil" (Genesis 3:5).

Catholics and most Christians read the second account of human creation in Genesis 2 in the context provided by Genesis 1, complementing the insight from that first account. Genesis 2:7 recounts that "then the LORD God formed man of dust from the ground, and breathed into his nostrils the breath of life; and man became a living being." This comparatively primitive picture shows God "playing with clay" and forming man (Hebrew *ha-adam*) from dirt from the ground (Hebrew *ha-adamah*), using a word play on the Hebrew words for man, *adam*, and ground, *adamah*. Into this clay model God breathes the breath of life, so that *adam* becomes a living being.

Neither the Hebrew nor any of its Greek and Latin translations use the word for "breath" that corresponds to *soul*. Yet even early reflection on this verse led interpreters to see in the primitive picture of God's breathing life into the clay a symbol of God's creating the human soul (as an independent action, "from nothing") within the body that had been formed from preexistent material. Thus man or *adam* is related both to the material earth and to God's divine life through his immaterial soul, which transcends the material earth.

This second creation account mentions that God put the human in a garden with wonderful trees, including the Tree of Life and the Tree of the Knowledge of Good and Evil. The Council of Trent, with later reaffirmation from Vatican II and the catechism based on it, makes this claim: "The Church, interpreting the symbolism of biblical language in an authentic way, in the light of the New Testament and Tradition, teaches that our first parents, Adam and Eve, were constituted in an original 'state of holiness and justice'" (Council of Trent, "On Original Sin").

After God put man in the garden, he commanded him, "You may freely eat of every tree of the garden; but of the tree of the knowledge of good and evil you shall not eat, for in the day that you eat of it you shall die" (Genesis 2:16-17). This commandment makes explicit what had till then been merely implicit: that although man ranks highest among and has widespread authority over earth's creatures, his authority is limited by God's explicit command prohibiting food from this one tree. God indicates the gravity of this command by threatening the penalty of death for disobedience.

Temptation and Fall

The woman, the partner whom God creates to relieve the man's loneliness, becomes the target of the serpent's temptation in Genesis 3. Whatever the primitive implications of the serpent and its associations with pagan fertility rites, the late Old Testament Book of Wisdom (2:24) and Revelation 12:9 identify this tempting serpent with Satan. His challenge is subtle and indirect: "Did God say, 'You shall not eat of any tree of the garden'?" (Genesis 3:1). The woman's response exaggerates God's command, "You shall not eat of the fruit of the tree...neither shall you touch it, lest you die" (3:3).

The serpent then openly challenges God's credibility: "You will not die. For God knows that when you eat of it your eyes will be opened, and you will be like God, knowing good and evil" (Genesis 3:4-5). In attempting to get humans to disbelieve and disregard God's threatened punishments, the serpent focuses on what is most galling to humans: the fact that they are not God but are dependent on God and subject to God's definition of good and evil.

This chafing at the limits imposed on his creaturehood by God will run through the entire history of man's sins and rebellions against his Creator. As the account in Genesis goes on to make clear, the effects of this sin (standing, as it were, for all sin) are devastating. Instead of accepting God's offered relationship of love as his sons and daughters, humans try to become autonomous and independent from God, determining for themselves what is right and wrong. This sets them up as rivals to God and, because God is obviously more powerful than they, leads them to fear and hide from God. Sin breaks our relationship with God and, as Genesis 3:12-19 indicates, also with other humans—especially pitting man and woman against each other. It breaks man's harmony with other material creatures, which now rebel against human authority as humans have rebelled against divine authority.

Redemption

This alienation of humans from God was so irreconcilable that only God could remove it. We have seen that the New Testament portrays the Son of God becoming man ("the Word became flesh," John 1:14) to undo man's disobedience by his own obedience unto death. John's Gospel goes on to identify this Word with the only Son of God (1:14b), who is also "the Lamb of God, who takes away the sin of the world" (1:29). The Johannine *midrashic* reflection on the Creation and Fall in Genesis goes far beyond the primeval "beginning" to the subsequent conflict with evil and consequent suffering of God's Incarnate Son and Word. However, John's prologue and Gospel provide a context and rationale for God's creative and saving activities in Genesis and beyond.

Paul's explanation of the reversal of Adam's sin by Christ is key to the Christian biblical understanding of sin and salvation:

> Have this mind among yourselves, which is yours in
> Christ Jesus, who, though he was in the form of God, did
> not count equality with God a thing to be grasped, but
> emptied himself, taking the form of a servant, being born
> in the likeness of men. And being found in human form
> he humbled himself and became obedient unto death,
> even death on a cross.
>
> PHILIPPIANS 2:5-8

As the Word made flesh, the Son of God reversed the human
tendency to grasp at equality with God by emptying himself
even of the equality with God he already had. Christ gave up
his divine prerogative to share humbly in our human condition as slaves bound to obedience to our Creator. So offensive was human disobedience and so drastic was the punishment requiring all humans to die that, to overcome it, God's
Son took on himself the death that we deserved. Thus he
overcame both sin and death by his love and obedience.

The curse on the serpent in Genesis 3:15 originally func-
tioned as an etiological story—that is, a story that explains
the origins of the contemporary antagonism between
snakes and humans and the widespread human repulsion
for snakes. "I will put enmity between you [the serpent]
and the woman, and between your seed and her seed; he
shall bruise your head, and you shall bruise his heel." But
the New Testament clearly sees in this story God's promise
of salvation, through the messianic seed of the woman,
from the evil effects of the satanic serpent. Thus Jesus
explains to his disciples in Luke:

> I saw Satan fall like lightning from heaven. Behold, I
> have given you authority to tread upon serpents and
> scorpions, and over all the power of the enemy; and
> nothing shall hurt you. Nevertheless do not rejoice in
> this, that the spirits are subject to you; but rejoice that
> your names are written in heaven.
>
> LUKE 10:18-20

The best known New Testament reference and response to the curse in Genesis 3:15 is in Revelation 12. There the satanic dragon (identified with the serpent in Genesis) tries to eat the messianic Son of the woman. However, through "the blood of the Lamb" (and of the martyrs, Revelation 12:11 tells us), Satan is expelled from his place as prosecuting attorney against humans at God's judgment seat. In his frustration and wrath he then persecutes the other children of the woman who follow her Son on earth (Revelation12:7-12, 17).

Conclusion

Thus we come full circle from our original questions, "Whence did we come? Where are we going?" Through looking at the "beginnings" in Genesis, as interpreted especially in the New Testament, patristic authors, and Church teachings, we have sketched a broad outline of the biblical worldview concerning God, humans, sin, and salvation. It is this biblical worldview as read through Catholic eyes that provides the context for a Catholic answer to the question, "What does the Bible say about the end times?" For the only adequate explanation of the frightening scenes of devastation and judgment in Revelation and other biblical apocalyptic texts and passages is in the context of divine judgment on human evil. But even the Book of Revelation, which so many readers find frightening, has at the center of its depictions of judgment the salvation brought to us sinners by the "Lamb who was slain" to atone for our sins and to reconcile us to God our Creator and Judge.

Notes:

1. William Watts, trans., *St. Augustine's Confessions*, Loeb Classical Library (Cambridge, Mass.: Harvard University Press, 1950), 2: "fecisti nos ad te et inquietum est cor nostrum, donec requiescat in te" (*Confessions* 1.1, my nonliteral translation for the plural sense).

2. See Anthony Kenny, *A Brief History of Western Philosophy* (Oxford; Malden, Mass.: Blackwell, 1998), 112: "First, [John] Philoponus attacked Aristotle's doctrine that the world had always existed. Some pagan philosophers were willing to accept that God was the creator of the world, in the sense that the world's existence had, from all eternity, been causally dependent on God. Others were prepared to accept that the world had had a beginning, in the sense that the orderly cosmos we know had, at a particular time, been brought out of chaos. But all the pagan philosophers of the time accepted the eternity of matter, and this, Christians believed, was incompatible with the Genesis account of the creation of heaven and earth out of nothing." Compare James B. Wilbur and Harold J. Allen, *The Worlds of the Early Greek Philosophers* (Buffalo, N.Y.: Prometheus, 1979), 8.

3. See Luke Timothy Johnson and William S. Kurz, S.J., *The Future of Catholic Biblical Scholarship: A Constructive Conversation* (Grand Rapids, Mich.: Eerdmans, 2002), 163-65.

4. Although the Greek translation (henceforth usually LXX) does not retain this distinction but simply uses the simple word for "to make" all through this creation account, the Latin translation on which the later Western church depended follows the Hebraic distinction between *create* and *make*.

5. See Isaiah 45:8, 12, 18; 48:7; 54:16; 65:17-18.

6. David Winston, "Solomon, Wisdom of," in David Noel Freedman et al., eds., *Anchor Bible Dictionary,* (New York: Doubleday, 1992), vol. 6, 120.

7. 4 Ezra's Jewish core sections were written about A.D. 90-120. The apocryphal work is also named 2 Esdras in some scholarly Bibles, but it is not accepted into the Catholic canon of the Bible. Compare Raymond Edward Brown, et. al., eds., *New Jerome Biblical Commentary* (London: Geoffrey Chapman, 1995), 1062.

8. *New Jerome Biblical Commentary*, 444. Since 2 Maccabees was written about 120-130 B.C., 2 Maccabees 7:28 is probably the "first biblical mention of 'creation *ex nihilo*.'" On creation *ex nihilo*, see Paul Copan, "Is *Creatio Ex Nihilo* a Post-Biblical Invention? An Examination of Gerhard May's Proposal," *Trinity Journal* 17.1 (Spring 1996), 77-93, reproduced online with permission at http://www.earlychurch.org.uk/article_exnihilo _copan.html, last accessed February 2004.

9. For example, Philo, *De confusione linguarum* 146: "And even if there be not as yet any one who is worthy to be called a son of God, nevertheless let him labour earnestly to be adorned according to his first-born word, the

eldest of his angels, as the great archangel of many names; for he is called the authority, and the name of God, and the Word, and man according to God's image, and he who sees Israel." In C.D. Yonge, *The Works of Philo Complete and Unabridged* (Peabody, Mass.: Hendrickson, 1993), 247.

10. Wisdom literature is quite difficult to date. The Book of Proverbs was published after the exile, close to 500 B.C., but some materials seem to go back to the period of the monarchy (ca. 1004-926 B.C.). Compare J. Terence Forestell, "Proverbs," *Jerome Biblical Commentary* (henceforth *JBC*) (Englewood Cliffs, N.J.: Prentice-Hall, 1968), 495.

11. Louis J. Puhl, S.J., *The Spiritual Exercises of St. Ignatius Based on Studies in the Language of the Autograph* (Chicago: Loyola University Press, 1951), section 23, p. 12).

12. Puhl, sections 136-48, pp. 60-63.

13. In the statement "You have made him little less than God," the RSV translation *God* is based on the Hebrew word for God (*Elohim*), which because of its plural form could be translated God or gods (or divine beings, later applied also to angels). To preserve the idea of the oneness of God the Jewish translators of the Greek Bible used the translation "angels," which the Latin translation from the Greek followed. But the alternate Latin translation that was based on the Hebrew text retained *God*.

14. For example, Origen noted that after quoting God's intention to "make man in our own image and likeness," Genesis mentions man's creation only "in the image of God." "Now the fact that he said 'he made him in the image of God' and was silent about the likeness points to nothing else but this, that man received the honor of God's image in his first creation, whereas the perfection of God's likeness was reserved for him at the consummation. The purpose of this was that man should acquire it for himself by his own earnest efforts to imitate God" (*On First Principles* 3.6.1, quoted in Andrew Louth with Marco Conti, eds., *Ancient Christian Commentary on Scripture, Old Testament I: Genesis 1-11* (Downers Grove, Ill.: InterVarsity, 2001), 29.

15. *Catechism of the Catholic Church*, 2nd ed. (Vatican: Libreria Editrice Vaticana, 1997 [Glossary and Index 2000]), henceforth *CCC*.

chapter two

The Prophets'
Eschatological Warnings:
Isaiah, Jeremiah, Ezekiel, and Daniel

We have seen that God did not abandon the human race when our first ancestors rebelled and tried to "be as God." The New Testament and later Christians interpreted the curse of the serpent in Genesis 3:15, "I will put enmity between you and the woman, and between your seed and her seed; he shall bruise your head, and you shall bruise his heel," as God's immediate promise that he would one day crush the satanic serpent through the messianic descendant of the woman. God's first step in restoring the human race came through Abraham: God chose a people with whom he made covenants in order to educate them in his ways. In turn, through Abraham's descendants "all the families of the earth shall bless themselves" (Genesis 12:3).

By Moses God rescued these Israelites from their slavery to the Egyptians and gave them another covenant, along with the Law and the Promised Land of Canaan. Scripture treats this Mosaic deliverance as the creation of the nation Israel, using motifs from creation narratives. For example, God's power overcomes the sea (at the Red Sea) to provide dry land (so the Israelites can cross) and then overwhelms their oppressors in the returning sea. As the song of Moses proclaims: "Who is like thee, O LORD, among the gods? Who is like thee, majestic in holiness, terrible in glorious deeds, doing wonders? Thou didst stretch out thy right hand, the earth swallowed them" (Exodus 15:11-12).

The plagues by which God sets Israel free from Egypt—water becoming blood, frogs, gnats, flies, pestilence, boils, hailstorms, locusts, darkness, and finally the killing of the Egyptian firstborn—provide symbols and imagery of God's wrath and deliverance from oppression in later prophetic and apocalyptic writing, including Revelation. The blood of the Passover lamb on the doorposts, through which the Israelite firstborn were spared God's punishment on the Egyptians, becomes a principal image for salvation not only in the Jewish Passover liturgy but in the Gospel of John and Revelation. Other Passover elements and symbols—such as unleavened bread, the angel of death, consecration of the firstborn, crossing of the Red Sea, pillar of cloud and pillar of fire, manna, forty years, the desert, and water from the rock—will also be reused heavily in later Jewish liturgy, psalms, and prophetic and apocalyptic writings.

After Moses' death, God, through Moses' disciple Joshua, led the Israelites in their conquest of the land. Through God's anointing and Spirit, "judges" like Deborah, Gideon, and Samson helped the Israelites overcome oppressors, until the last judge, Samuel, anointed the first king, Saul, at the people's request. After rejecting the disobedient Saul as king, God made a royal covenant with David, who ruled on Mount Zion. The language of God's adoption of David and his heirs, "You are my son, today I have begotten you" (Psalm 2:7), which eventually was applied to the expected Messiah, resonate with God's original offer of adoption and kingship over creation that was implied in his creating Adam in a position of dominion over other material creatures.

David's son Solomon became a biblical model of wisdom in an era of peace and prosperity. Solomon built the temple on Zion. Zion and its temple in turn became a symbol of the created universe, so that God's presence there symbolized his presence on earth with his people.[1] However, after

Solomon's death, the ten northern tribes of Israel rebelled against the oppressive reign of the later Davidic kings in the southern tribe of Judah to form a second nation. Because both nations, Israel and Judah, continued to sin against God and to break his covenants and law, God raised up prophets among both to warn the people to amend their ways and return to him.

The historical books of the Pentateuch, as well as Judges, 1 and 2 Samuel, and 1 and 2 Kings, read like a constant refrain of God's offers and calls and the people's sins and their punishment through oppression by other nations. When they repent, God rescues them, but soon their descendants are backsliding again. As the people of both Israel and Judah multiply their sins against God and his law and covenants, the warnings of the prophets become increasingly dire and threatening.

The language of prophetic judgment and warnings provides much of the vocabulary and imagery that will be used in apocalyptic writings about the end times. Isaiah, Ezekiel, Jeremiah, and Daniel especially contain vivid passages about God's wrath and threatened punishments that will color much of the wording of the visions and prophecies of the Book of Revelation. Let us briefly look at some of these prophetic warnings, beginning with Isaiah.

Prophetic Warnings in Isaiah

Most scholars recognize that the Book of Isaiah contains several levels of material, from early prophecies while the kingdom of Judah was still standing to later material pertaining to the exile and perhaps after. However, subsequent biblical writers and figures, including even Jesus, treat the Book of Isaiah as a unified biblical whole, as it now stands in the canon of Scripture. We shall generally do likewise, especially since our main concern is how prophecies and visions in Isaiah provide much of the language and imagery with which Revelation and other biblical writings about the end times express visions and prophecies.

God's Judgment and Mercy

The prophet Isaiah dates his visions during the reigns of Kings Uzziah and Jotham (around 750 to 735 B.C.), and Ahaz and Hezekiah (734 to 686 B.C.) (see Isaiah 1:1). Isaiah's very first vision begins with God's bitter complaint about the rebellion of Israel against their Father and Creator: "Sons have I reared and brought up, but they have rebelled against me. The ox knows its owner, and the ass its master's crib; but Israel does not know, my people does not understand" (Isaiah 1:2-3). So sinful have been God's people that "if the LORD of hosts had not left us a few survivors, we should have been like Sodom, and become like Gomorrah" (Isaiah 1:9). Even this early prophetic complaint reuses still earlier stories from Genesis—about the destruction of the infamous cities of Sodom and Gomorrah—in order to accentuate the severity of God's judgment.

Other complaints in Isaiah will be echoed in Revelation, such as his comparison of Jerusalem to a harlot: "How the faithful city has become a harlot, she that was full of justice! Righteousness lodged in her, but now murderers" (Isaiah 1:21). Nevertheless, God does not simply desert his people but promises either redemption or punishment, depending on how they respond to his offers: "Zion shall be redeemed by justice, and those in her who repent, by righteousness. But rebels and sinners shall be destroyed together, and those who forsake the LORD shall be consumed" (Isaiah 1:27-28). From Genesis to Revelation, Scripture consistently announces the two possible outcomes of salvation and punishment that result from the human choice either to repent or to remain hardened in sin.

In the next recorded message in Isaiah, God delineates the role of Mount Zion in the final days. This promise will play a prominent role in later visions and prophecies about the end times, up to and including those in Revelation.

> It shall come to pass in the latter days that the mountain of the house of the LORD shall be established as the highest of the mountains, and shall be raised above the hills; and all the nations shall flow to it, and many peoples shall come, and say: "Come, let us go up to the mountain of the LORD, to the house of the God of Jacob; that he may teach us his ways and that we may walk in his paths." For out of Zion shall go forth the law, and the word of the LORD from Jerusalem. He shall judge between the nations, and shall decide for many peoples; and they shall beat their swords into plowshares, and their spears into pruning hooks; nation shall not lift up sword against nation, neither shall they learn war any more.
>
> ISAIAH 2:2-4

These plans of God for Zion evidently do not coincide with human plans, for they reject both war and political domination. Instead Zion is to be the focal point for the entire world to learn about God's ways. Zion is to be the source of worldwide peace based on God's law.

Whatever God's plans may be for Zion in the final days, the people of Jerusalem and Judah during the time of Isaiah are refusing to live as God wants. God's response to them is the famous song of the vineyard. After God planted and nurtured his special vine, "he looked for it to yield grapes, but it yielded wild grapes" (Isaiah 5:2b). What more could God do for his vineyard, for his people? God looked for justice, but they produced bloodshed (5:7b). Therefore God allows the northern kingdom of Israel to be taken into exile, with a similar fate threatening the southern kingdom of Judah.

"A Man of Unclean Lips"
At the end of King Uzziah's reign, which also marks the end

of the first part of Isaiah's ministry, Isaiah reports a momentous revelation that he had of God on his throne, a vision that will influence the description of later visions of God on his throne in Ezekiel 1:4–2:1, Daniel 7, and Revelation 4–5:

> In the year that King Uzziah died I saw the Lord sitting upon a throne, high and lifted up; and his train filled the temple. Above him stood the seraphim; each had six wings: with two he covered his face, and with two he covered his feet, and with two he flew.
>
> Isaiah 6:1-2

In this vision God's heavenly throne is closely related to the temple (which God's train filled). The six-winged seraphim (in various forms as diverse heavenly figures) will influence visions of later biblical writers. They symbolize members of the heavenly court, who stand before God's throne. Their song of worship continues to be echoed in Orthodox and Catholic Eucharistic liturgies (which are thus perceived as joining the heavenly worship of God) to this day: "Holy, holy, holy is the LORD of hosts; the whole earth is full of his glory" (Isaiah 6:3b).

The vision arouses awe and dread in the prophet. "And I said: 'Woe is me! For I am lost; for I am a man of unclean lips, and I dwell in the midst of a people of unclean lips; for my eyes have seen the King, the LORD of hosts!'" (Isaiah 6:5). The prophet recoils, aware of his own uncleanness and lack of holiness. He knows that in the presence of the Holy God, his uncleanness threatens even his life.

Such fears of seeing God were common among the Israelites: "So Jacob called the name of the place Peniel, saying, 'For I have seen God face to face, and yet my life is preserved'" (Genesis 32:30; see Genesis 16:13; Exodus 3:6; Deuteronomy 5:24; Judges 13:22). Later, in the Sermon on the Mount, Jesus will promise a circumstance in which one may see God without fear: "Blessed are the pure in heart, for they shall see God" (Matthew 5:8). The prologue of the Gospel of John definitively challenges the claims of all Old Testament theophanies (visions of God): "No one has ever seen God; the only Son, who is in the bosom of the Father, he has made him known" (John 1:18; see 1 John 4:12).

God responds to the prophet's fear regarding his uncleanness in a way that many might find surprising. God does not deny Isaiah's uncleanness with some assurance based on popular psychology, such as "I'm OK, you're OK." God is a God of truth. He has one of the seraphim apply a burning coal to Isaiah's mouth: "Behold, this has touched your lips; your guilt is taken away, and your sin forgiven" (Isaiah 6:7b). God's answer to our human uncleanness is to cleanse us.

Then God asks for a volunteer to send, and Isaiah responds, "Here am I! Send me" (Isaiah 6:8b). God's commission to Isaiah is a sobering one: "Go, and say to this people: 'Hear and hear, but do not understand; see and see, but do not perceive.' Make the heart of this people fat, and their ears heavy, and shut their eyes; lest they see with their eyes, and hear with their ears, and understand with their hearts, and turn and be healed" (6:9b-10). Isaiah is to persist in his apparently fruitless mission "until cities lie waste without inhabitant, and houses without men, and the land is utterly desolate, and the LORD removes men far away" (6:11b-12a). New Testament authors repeatedly refer to this grim mission of Isaiah, as Gospel writers and others struggle to understand the traumatic destruction in A.D. 70 of Jerusalem and the temple, the center of their world and the previously privileged site of God's presence among them.

The "Isaiah Apocalypse"

Chapters 24 through 27 of Isaiah are often referred to as the "Isaiah Apocalypse." They form a transitional genre of writing between prophecy and apocalyptic. They focus on such themes as general judgment, an eschatological banquet, and signs in heaven, which become standard emphases in later apocalyptic writings, including Revelation. The chapters presuppose extreme national humiliation (probably originally under Assyria) and look to God to overcome the devastation, which they portray in terms of primeval forces of chaos such as the dragon or Leviathan.

Isaiah 24 begins by attributing to the Lord himself the desolation of "the land" (a term that probably initially referred to Israel but later readers would expand to include the entire earth). "The earth mourns...the heavens languish together with the earth.... For they have transgressed the laws...broken the everlasting covenant" (Isaiah 24:4, 5). Then comes God's judgment on sinners (mythically described as in both heaven and on earth): "On that day the LORD will punish the host of heaven, in heaven, and the kings of the earth, on the earth" (24:21).

The judgment is portrayed as affecting even the moon and sun: "Then the moon will be confounded, and the sun ashamed; for the LORD of hosts will reign on Mount Zion and in Jerusalem and before his elders he will manifest his glory" (24:23). In Isaiah 27:1 God's judgment and victory over chaotic forces is symbolized as his victory over the primeval Leviathan and dragon in the sea: "In that day the LORD with his hard and great and strong sword will punish Leviathan the fleeing serpent, Leviathan the twisting serpent, and he will slay the dragon that is in the sea."

After the judgment comes an eschatological feast on Mount Zion:

> On this mountain the LORD of hosts will make for all peoples a feast of fat things, a feast of wine on the lees.... And he will destroy on this mountain the covering that is cast over all peoples, the veil that is spread over all nations. He will swallow up death for ever, and the Lord

> GOD will wipe away tears from all faces, and the reproach
> of his people he will take away from all the earth.
>
> ISAIAH 25:6-8

In the end times (see Revelation 7:17; 21:4), God's wiping away our tears will be a prominent symbol of his definitive salvation.

Isaiah 40–55

Chapters 40–55 of Isaiah apparently stem from the time of the exile after the fall of Judah. Even when God allows his people to be punished for their refusal to keep their covenant with him and to obey him, he does not abandon them. He raises up another prophet in the spirit of Isaiah to encourage them not to give up hope in their Lord and Creator. After comforting his people, God instructs the prophet to tell Jerusalem "that her iniquity is pardoned, that she has received from the LORD's hand double for all her sins" (Isaiah 40:2).

The Gospels of Matthew, Mark, and Luke repeat the next part of this message as their introduction to Jesus' public ministry. John the Baptist will repeat Isaiah 40:3-5:

> A voice cries: "In the wilderness prepare the way of the LORD, make straight in the desert a highway for our God. Every valley shall be lifted up, and every mountain and hill be made low; the uneven ground shall become level, and the rough places a plain. And the glory of the LORD shall be revealed, and all flesh shall see it together."

Isaiah 40:12-31 emphasizes that God is Creator of the universe. Who has instructed God? Before God "the nations are like a drop from a bucket...as the dust on the scales" (40:15). Isaiah mocks idols as lifeless and useless. God also controls history and "brings princes to nought, and makes the rulers of the earth as nothing" (40:23). He calls the stars by name. No one can hide from God's knowledge.

The next two chapters depict primarily a lawsuit that God initiates against the nations. As Creator of the entire world, God has raised up a Persian leader, Cyrus, to wreak vengeance on the Babylonians, who sent the Israelites into exile. "Who stirred up one from the east whom victory meets at every step? He gives up nations before him, so that he tramples kings under foot..." (41:2). "I, the LORD, the first, and with the last; I am He" (41:4b). Revelation will similarly use the titles "the first and the last," both for God and for Jesus, to emphasize their universal dominion and eternal existence (Revelation 1:17; 2:8; 22:13).

Although many nations will dread Cyrus' string of conquests, God gives special assurance to his people:

> But you, Israel, my servant, Jacob, whom I have chosen, the offspring of Abraham, my friend; you whom I took from the ends of the earth, and called from its farthest corners, saying to you, "You are my servant, I have chosen you and not cast you off"; fear not, for I am with you, be not dismayed, for I am your God; I will strengthen you, I will help you, I will uphold you with my victorious right hand.
>
> ISAIAH 41:8-10

God is granting world conquests to a contemporary secular ruler, Cyrus, not to Israel. However, God is concurrently taking care of Israel through this same Cyrus, who will allow the Jews to return to their homeland and rebuild their temple.

Meanwhile, it is enough for Israel to know that their God has the power to provide for their needs, even miraculously:

> When the poor and needy seek water, and there is none, and their tongue is parched with thirst, I the LORD will answer them, I the God of Israel will not forsake them. I will open rivers on the bare heights, and fountains in the midst of the valleys; I will make the wilderness a pool of water, and the dry land springs of water...that men may

see and know, may consider and understand together, that the hand of the Lᴏʀᴅ has done this, the Holy One of Israel has created it.

Isaiah 41:17-20

The Servant Songs

Four "Servant Songs" that will be quite influential for the New Testament understanding of Jesus' identity and saving work occur in Isaiah 42–53. The servant may stand for Israel collectively, for a specially chosen individual, or (as he has often been interpreted through the ages) for both. The New Testament will generally identify the servant with Jesus, as in the first song:

Behold my servant, whom I uphold, my chosen, in whom my soul delights; I have put my Spirit upon him, he will bring forth justice to the nations. He will not cry or lift up his voice, or make it heard in the street; a bruised reed he will not break, and a dimly burning wick he will not quench; he will faithfully bring forth justice. He will not fail or be discouraged till he has established justice in the earth; and the coastlands wait for his law.

Isaiah 42:1-4

This provides some biblical context for understanding the emphasis in the Gospels on how much Jesus reached out to outcasts and sinners.

The second Servant Song, in Isaiah 49:1-6, will be pivotal for New Testament presentations of Jesus. It emphasizes the servant's call from the womb and clarifies that his mission is directed not only to Israel but, as a light, to all the nations. Even if the servant is originally interpreted as Israel, this song reaffirms the basic Old Testament truth that God's choice of the people Israel was not only for their sake but that they might be God's instrument for saving the whole world.

> The LORD called me from the womb, from the body of my mother he named my name. He made my mouth like a sharp sword, in the shadow of his hand he hid me; he made me a polished arrow, in his quiver he hid me away. And he said to me, "You are my servant, Israel, in whom I will be glorified." But I said, "I have labored in vain, I have spent my strength for nothing and vanity; yet surely my right is with the LORD, and my recompense with my God." And now the LORD says, who formed me from the womb to be his servant, to bring Jacob back to him, and that Israel might be gathered to him, for I am honored in the eyes of the LORD, and my God has become my strength—he says: "It is too light a thing that you should be my servant to raise up the tribes of Jacob and to restore the preserved of Israel; I will give you as a light to the nations, that my salvation may reach to the end of the earth."

> ISAIAH 49:1b-6

Christians also apply the third Servant Song (Isaiah 50:4-11) to Jesus, especially as he is rejected by his own people in his passion. Some of its details, like Jesus' obedience to God his Father, as well as the shame and spitting that he endured, are emphasized in the Gospel accounts of Jesus' passion and crucifixion.

> The Lord GOD has opened my ear, and I was not rebellious, I turned not backward. I gave my back to the smiters, and my cheeks to those who pulled out the beard; I hid not my face from shame and spitting. For the Lord GOD helps me; therefore I have not been confounded; therefore I have set my face like a flint, and I know that I shall not be put to shame.

> ISAIAH 50:5-7

The fourth Servant Song (Isaiah 52:13–53:12) became a central passage for New Testament writers to understand the significance of Jesus' passion in light of God's plans to save the human race that has become alienated from him:

> Behold, my servant shall prosper, he shall be exalted and lifted up, and shall be very high. As many were astonished at him—his appearance was so marred, beyond human semblance, and his form beyond that of the sons of men—so shall he startle many nations.... Who has believed what we have heard? And to whom has the arm of the LORD been revealed? For he grew up before him like a young plant, and like a root out of dry ground; he had no form or comeliness that we should look at him, and no beauty that we should desire him. He was despised and rejected by men; a man of sorrows, and acquainted with grief; and as one from whom men hide their faces he was despised, and we esteemed him not.
>
> ISAIAH 52:13-15, 53:1-3

The most surprising aspect of this message of the Servant Songs is that God will overcome the pervasive evil of the human race not primarily through divine judgment, wrath, and punishment but through someone's willingly succumbing to the evil and bearing it on behalf of sinners:

> Surely he has borne our griefs and carried our sorrows; yet we esteemed him stricken, smitten by God, and afflicted. But he was wounded for our transgressions, he was bruised for our iniquities; upon him was the chastisement that made us whole, and with his stripes we are healed. All we like sheep have gone astray; we have turned every one to his own way; and the LORD has laid on him the iniquity of us all.
>
> ISAIAH 53:4-6

The suffering of the servant is not deserved. He, though innocent, is suffering on behalf of us, the guilty, and in our place. The song goes on to portray the suffering servant in terms of a sacrificial lamb, who dies without protest that we might be allowed to keep living:

> He was oppressed, and he was afflicted, yet he opened not his mouth; like a lamb that is led to the slaughter, and like a sheep that before its shearers is dumb, so he opened not his mouth. By oppression and judgment he was taken away; and as for his generation, who considered that he was cut off out of the land of the living, stricken for the transgression of my people? And they made his grave with the wicked and with a rich man in his death, although he had done no violence, and there was no deceit in his mouth. Yet it was the will of the LORD to bruise him; he has put him to grief.
>
> ISAIAH 53:7-10a

The passion accounts emphasize many of the details from this Servant Song and use them to describe Jesus' suffering. This is one way in which the passion narratives demonstrate "that Christ died for our sins in accordance with the scriptures" (1 Corinthians 15:3). The comparison to a lamb led to the slaughter will reappear in the reference to Jesus as "Lamb of God" in John 1:29 and 1:36 and as "the Lamb who was slain" in Revelation 5:12 and 13:8.

The Servant Song ends on a note of vindication for the servant who made himself "an offering for sin" (Isaiah 53:10, see vv. 11-12). Jesus' vindication will surpass any vindication imagined by this prophetic song, for "he was raised on the third day in accordance with the scriptures" (1 Corinthians 15:4).

Within the Book of Isaiah, the "Book of Consolation" (Isaiah 40–55) ends with a powerful poem of consolation. God invites "every one who thirsts, come to the waters" (Isaiah 55:1). Come to be fed by God, even those who have no money. "Why do you spend your money for that which is not bread, and your labor for that which does not satisfy? Hearken diligently to me, and eat what is good" (55:2). God invites us to come to him for all our needs, to heed his word and his revelation: "I will make with you an everlasting covenant, my steadfast, sure love for David" (55:3). God calls the people to repent and return to his ways of living. "For my thoughts are not your thoughts, neither are your ways my ways, says the LORD" (55:8). God's word will achieve that which it is sent to do, as surely as rain waters the earth (see 55:10-11).

Zion and the New Jerusalem

Most of the material in Isaiah 56–66 seems to originate after the exile. Isaiah 56:7 promises that the restored temple on "my holy mountain" (Zion) will benefit all nations: "For my house shall be called a house of prayer for all peoples." Through the prophets God continues to rebuke (as in Ezekiel 34) Judah's "shepherds," her political and religious leaders, for failing to provide pastoral oversight for their people, who continue to engage in false and forbidden worship. God reassures those who are suffering that he will forgive their sins if they repent (see Isaiah 57:14-21).

Isaiah 60 prophesies a glorious restoration of Jerusalem and Mount Zion, to which nations will come bringing "gold and frankincense" and other gifts (Isaiah 60:6). Restored Zion will exceed Solomon's city. Instead of the sun and the moon, God's glory will provide light (Isaiah 60:19), just as in Revelation 21:23, "the city has no need of sun or moon to shine upon it, for the glory of God is its light, and its lamp is the Lamb."

As later Old Testament and New Testament prophets and apocalyptic writers imagine the end times, a glorified picture of Zion repeatedly plays a major role. Zion often symbolizes the new creation at the end of time. This enables apocalyptic writings like Revelation to portray the end times in terms that refer back to God's creation "in the beginning." Isaiah 61 includes still another poem, similar to the Servant Songs, of a mission to Zion:

> The Spirit of the Lord GOD is upon me, because the LORD has anointed me to bring good tidings to the afflicted; he has sent me to bind up the brokenhearted, to proclaim liberty to the captives, and the opening of the prison to those who are bound; to proclaim the year of the LORD's favor, and the day of vengeance of our God; to comfort all who mourn; to grant to those who mourn in Zion—to give them a garland instead of ashes.
>
> ISAIAH 61:1-3

Foreigners will help rebuild Zion's ruins, and the people "shall be called the priests of the LORD" (61:6). This poem reverts to marital imagery to portray God's love for his bride Zion: "You shall be a crown of beauty in the hand of the LORD" (62:3), "no more be termed Forsaken" (62:4), "but you shall be called My delight is in her, and your land Married; for the LORD delights in you, and your land shall be married.... As the bridegroom rejoices over the bride, so shall your God rejoice over you" (62:4, 5). God's love for Zion will be manifest in the end times in terms of the most intimate form of love known to humans.

The Book of Jeremiah

Jeremiah prophesied from 627 to after 580 B.C. (his life probably ending in Egyptian exile). He emphasized rewards and punishment that correspond respectively to faithfulness to God or disobedience and worship of other gods. After the catastrophic fall of Jerusalem happened as he had prophesied and warned, Jeremiah's prophecy changed its emphasis to hope and promised a new and lasting covenant with God.

Prophetic Call

Jeremiah's call to be a prophet becomes the model for Paul's description of his own calling (see Galatians 1:15). "Before I formed you in the womb I knew you, and before you were born I consecrated you; I appointed you a prophet to the nations" (Jeremiah 1:5). God reassures the prophet:

> Do not say, "I am only a youth"; for to all to whom I send you you shall go, and whatever I command you you shall speak. Be not afraid of them, for I am with you to deliver you, says the LORD.
>
> JEREMIAH 1:7-8

Jeremiah's mission is not limited to Israel. It will affect all nations, for God is God of the whole world, not only of Israel: "Behold, I have put my words in your mouth. See, I have set you this day over nations and over kingdoms, to pluck up and to break down, to destroy and to overthrow, to build and to plant" (1:9b-10).

Jeremiah is called to condemn Israel's apostasies and to exhort the people to repent of their harlotry with other lovers (gods). The false bride Judah (the southern kingdom) followed the harmful example of her sister Israel (the northern kingdom) in committing adultery against God (Jeremiah 2–3). Judgment is coming for the people's many sins; not even the temple can save Judah (Jeremiah 4–7). The people should put no false hope in the temple's presence among them, for only if they amend their ways will God let them continue to dwell in their land: "Has this house, which is called by my name, become a den of robbers in your eyes?" (Jeremiah 7:11). As God has allowed his shrine at Shiloh to be demolished, he threatens the same destruction for the temple: "Therefore I will do to the house which is called by my name, and in which you trust, and to the place which I gave to you and to your fathers, as I did to Shiloh" (7:14).

A salient aspect of the message of the prophets is the

way in which it counteracts the current mood of the people. When the people are complacent and abandon God's ways, the prophets threaten punishment to come. After the people begin their punishment in exile, when they are tempted to despair, the prophet preaches consolation and hope. Thus, after Judah is conquered and her people exiled, Jeremiah 30–31 delivers consolation and a promise from God that she will be restored. God will punish her but not destroy her: "I will make a full end of all the nations among whom I scattered you, but of you I will not make a full end. I will chasten you in just measure, and I will by no means leave you unpunished" (Jeremiah 30:11).

God will forgive the people's sins because of his love for them: "I have loved you with an everlasting love; therefore I have continued my faithfulness to you. Again I will build you, and you shall be built, O virgin Israel!" (Jeremiah 31:3b-4a). Jeremiah proclaims to the nations that God will bring Israel back from dispersion:

> Hear the word of the LORD, O nations, and declare it in the coastlands afar off; say, "He who scattered Israel will gather him, and will keep him as a shepherd keeps his flock." For the LORD has ransomed Jacob, and has redeemed him from hands too strong for him.
>
> JEREMIAH 31:10-11

Folk maxims about children suffering for the sins of their fathers will no longer be applicable to Israel:

> In those days they shall no longer say: "The fathers have eaten sour grapes, and the children's teeth are set on edge." But every one shall die for his own sin; each man who eats sour grapes, his teeth shall be set on edge.
>
> JEREMIAH 31:29-30; see also EZEKIEL 18:2-20

Each person bears responsibility for his or her own choices.

The New Covenant in Jeremiah

The Old Testament chronicles how the people of God failed to keep every covenant that God made with them, thus exposing the nation to his fitting punishment. Jeremiah now promises a new covenant for the end times that will not be written on stone tablets but on the hearts of the people. This new covenant will be so interiorized that people will be less likely to experience it as an external restriction on their freedom in the form of a command by a superior (even God). Humans have chafed at every command of God, beginning with the first command to Adam and Eve, and continuing with each covenant that God has made with his people.

> Behold, the days are coming, says the LORD, when I will make a new covenant with the house of Israel and the house of Judah, not like the covenant which I made with their fathers when I took them by the hand to bring them out of the land of Egypt, my covenant which they broke, though I was their husband, says the LORD. But this is the covenant which I will make with the house of Israel after those days, says the LORD: I will put my law within them, and I will write it upon their hearts; and I will be their God, and they shall be my people.
>
> JEREMIAH 31:31-33

Such a covenant is portrayed as an ideal characteristic of future times of fulfillment (the end times), when Israel's sin will be overcome by love and obedience to her merciful God.

The New Testament will apply this prophecy to the new covenant through Jesus, interpreting the time from Jesus' first coming onward as the end times or the last days. For example, in the Acts of the Apostles, Peter's Pentecost application of Joel's prophecy provides a clear example of the New Testament distinction between the "last days" that are inaugurated by the risen Christ's sending of the Holy Spirit and the very "Last Day," when Christ will return in glory for judgment:

> And in the last days it shall be, God declares, that I will
> pour out my Spirit upon all flesh.... And I will show won-
> ders in the heaven above and signs on the earth beneath,
> blood, and fire, and vapor of smoke; the sun shall be
> turned into darkness and the moon into blood, before the
> day of the Lord comes, the great and manifest day.
>
> Acts 2:17, 19-20

As the Books of Isaiah and Ezekiel have included oracles
condemning foreign nations (Isaiah 13–23 and Ezekiel
25–32), so does the Book of Jeremiah (Jeremiah 46–51).
Isaiah portrayed Assyria as an instrument by which God
punished the northern kingdom Israel (by sending it into
exile), but he threatened that in turn God would punish
Assyria for its excessive cruelty and pride (Isaiah 10:5-15).
Especially relevant for later depictions of the end times, as
in Revelation, are Jeremiah's extensive condemnations of
Babylon (Jeremiah 51), which is God's instrument to punish the southern kingdom of Judah: "Babylon was a golden
cup in the Lord's hand, making all the earth drunken; the
nations drank of her wine, therefore the nations went mad"
(Jeremiah 51:7). Jeremiah prophesies that the kings of the
Medes will in turn punish Babylon for destroying God's
temple: "The Lord has stirred up the spirit of the kings of the
Medes, because his purpose concerning Babylon is to
destroy it, for that is the vengeance of the Lord, the
vengeance for his temple" (51:11).

Thus, although God used Babylon as his "hammer and
weapon of war," now he will destroy it for the evil it has
done in Zion. As Creator, God often uses human institutions
to achieve his goals in history. However, when the cruelty of
God's instruments exceeds the punishment that God
intended them to administer, he will punish them in turn.

> You are my hammer and weapon of war: with you I
> break nations in pieces; with you I destroy kingdoms;

with you I break in pieces the horse and his rider; with you I break in pieces the chariot and the charioteer.... I will requite Babylon and all the inhabitants of Chaldea before your very eyes for all the evil that they have done in Zion, says the LORD.

JEREMIAH 51:20-21, 24

As a result of God's punishment, Babylon, like Assyria, is about to become a byword of horror. "How Babylon is taken, the praise of the whole earth seized! How Babylon has become a horror among the nations!" (Jeremiah 51:41).

Then the heavens and the earth, and all that is in them, shall sing for joy over Babylon; for the destroyers shall come against them out of the north, says the LORD. Babylon must fall for the slain of Israel, as for Babylon have fallen the slain of all the earth.

JEREMIAH 51:48-49

Images of the waters of pre-creation chaos are applied to the Lord's destruction of Babylon (historically through the Medes):

Hark! a cry from Babylon! The noise of great destruction from the land of the Chaldeans! For the LORD is laying Babylon waste, and stilling her mighty voice. Their waves roar like many waters, the noise of their voice is raised; for a destroyer has come upon her, upon Babylon; her warriors are taken, their bows are broken in pieces; for the LORD is a God of recompense, he will surely requite.... Thus says the LORD of hosts: The broad wall of Babylon shall be leveled to the ground and her high gates shall be burned with fire.

JEREMIAH 51:54-56, 58a

Reverberations of Babylon's punishment will echo in Revelation. There the seer will describe the punishment of his "Babylon," the Roman Empire.

The Book of Ezekiel

Many bizarre components of the visions and the commissioning of Ezekiel as prophet seem to have influenced the accounts of visions and prophetic calls in later prophetic and apocalyptic writings, especially in Daniel and Revelation. Descriptions of visions of God in Ezekiel go out of their way to acknowledge God's transcendence. The combination of Ezekiel's vivid images and symbols, with his emphasis on God's awe-inspiring transcendence, apparently had a profound effect on how later prophets and seers would describe their comparable visions and experiences of God.

The Book of Ezekiel begins with the reference, customary in prophetic books, to the date, place, and situation in which he received his visions from God. Ezekiel was among the exiles from Judah at the Babylonian River Chebar when God revealed himself to him. He articulates this experience in the same way that most prophets have: "The word of the LORD came to Ezekiel the priest." This formula for prophecy emphasizes the message from God to the prophet. Ezekiel also refers to his feeling a divine compulsion: "And the hand of the LORD was upon him there" (Ezekiel 1:3). Ezekiel proceeds to describe in vivid detail his vision.

God's Chariot Throne

Many elements of Ezekiel's famous vision of God's chariot throne will be reapplied in describing the analogous throne vision in Revelation 4 and 5. Ezekiel's portrayal of this vision seems to be influenced in turn by descriptions of visions of the earlier prophets Micaiah—"I saw the LORD sitting on his throne, and all the host of heaven standing beside him" (1 Kings 22:19)—and Isaiah—"I saw the Lord sitting upon a throne.... Above him stood the seraphim" (Isaiah 6:1, 2). But whereas the accounts of the visions of Micaiah and Isaiah simply claimed that the prophet saw the Lord sitting on his throne, Ezekiel goes to almost inconceivable lengths to avoid even remotely hinting that he saw the Lord directly.

Before Ezekiel describes the throne and its occupant, he focuses on "the likeness of four living creatures" (Ezekiel 1:5), which from his description alone are hard to visualize. They had the form of men but with four faces and four wings. They had human hands under their wings on their four sides. The four faces were those of a man in front, a lion on the right, an ox on the left, and an eagle on the back (1:5-10). Ezekiel then adds that each creature had a wheel within a wheel with rims full of eyes. The wheels went wherever the living creatures went, "for the spirit of the living creatures was in the wheels" (1:20).

Over the living creatures was "the likeness of a firmament" (Ezekiel 1:22). "And above the firmament over their heads there was the likeness of a throne, in appearance like sapphire; and seated above the likeness of a throne was a likeness as it were of a human form" (1:26). To respect God's transcendence, Ezekiel does not say that he saw a throne but "the likeness of a throne;" he does not say that he saw a human form but "a likeness as it were of a human form."

This same indirection continues in Ezekiel's description of the appearance of this human form:

> And upward from what had the appearance of his loins I saw as it were gleaming bronze, like the appearance of fire enclosed round about; and downward from what had the appearance of his loins I saw as it were the appearance of fire, and there was brightness round about him. Like the appearance of the bow that is in the cloud on the day of rain, so was the appearance of the brightness round about.
>
> EZEKIEL 1:27-28a

This indirection has multiple levels in Ezekiel's summary of his vision of the figure on the throne. "Such was the appearance of the likeness of the glory of the LORD. And when I saw it, I fell upon my face, and I heard the voice of one speaking" (Ezekiel 1:28b). Ezekiel does not maintain that he saw the Lord. He does not even claim to see the appearance of the Lord nor even the likeness of the Lord. What he claims to have seen is the appearance of the likeness of the glory of the Lord.

This indirection embodies an important truth: No human on earth can actually see God and remain alive in his or her earthly body, for God's infinite being is too much for our limited nature to bear. The vision that Ezekiel saw was not God himself but only "the appearance of the likeness of the glory" of God. This makes a significant point about all descriptions of visions of divine realities, both in Scripture and in accounts of saints and visionaries.

Divine realities transcend the ability of ordinary human vision or imagination to grasp or fully express. When a seer like Ezekiel or John of Revelation describes the visions that he has seen, he must try to approximate what he experienced with the help of images and symbols from human sensation combined by imagination. He also must express what he saw in words from the particular human language in which he is writing. To depict such essentially indescribable experiences, a prophet or visionary will naturally use expressions familiar to him from earlier, comparable biblical prophetic and visionary writings. Thus Ezekiel uses but modifies wording from Isaiah to describe the visions that he has, as the prophet John of Revelation will in turn utilize but modify expressions from Ezekiel to describe his analogous visions.

The Call of Ezekiel

Ezekiel's call came directly out of his initial vision of "the appearance of the likeness of the glory of the LORD" on his throne (Ezekiel 1:28b). The divine voice told the prophet, "Son of man, stand upon your feet, and I will speak with you" (2:1). "And when he spoke to me, the Spirit entered into me and set me upon my feet; and I heard him speaking to me" (2:2).

The mission that God gives Ezekiel comes with a warning similar to that which he gave Isaiah and Jeremiah. God warns Ezekiel from the first that the people probably will not listen to his message:

> And he said to me, "Son of man, I send you to the people of Israel, to a nation of rebels, who have rebelled against me; they and their fathers have transgressed against me to this very day. The people also are impudent and stubborn: I send you to them; and you shall say to them, 'Thus says the Lord GOD.' And whether they hear or refuse to hear (for they are a rebellious house) they will know that there has been a prophet among them."
>
> EZEKIEL 2:3-5

Reassuring Ezekiel, the Lord asks him to deliver his message faithfully, whether or not the people heed it:

> And you, son of man, be not afraid of them, nor be afraid of their words, though briers and thorns are with you and you sit upon scorpions; be not afraid of their words, nor be dismayed at their looks, for they are a rebellious house. And you shall speak my words to them, whether they hear or refuse to hear; for they are a rebellious house.
>
> EZEKIEL 2:6-7

God warns Ezekiel not to be like the people but to obey him and eat the written scroll that he gives him. When he eats the scroll it is "in [his] mouth as sweet as honey" (3:3b). God then stiffens Ezekiel's resolve to speak the message to an unwilling audience (3:4-11).

The Vision of the Watchman
In a follow-up vision seven days later, God uses the image of

a watchman to describe Ezekiel's prophetic mission (see also Hosea 9:8; Isaiah 21:6-12; 52:8; 56:10; 62:6; Jeremiah 6:17):

> Son of man, I have made you a watchman for the house of Israel; whenever you hear a word from my mouth, you shall give them warning from me. If I say to the wicked, "You shall surely die," and you give him no warning, nor speak to warn the wicked from his wicked way, in order to save his life, that wicked man shall die in his iniquity; but his blood I will require at your hand. But if you warn the wicked, and he does not turn from his wickedness, or from his wicked way, he shall die in his iniquity; but you will have saved your life.
>
> EZEKIEL 3:17-19

The prophet has an obligation to warn his listeners when they are sinning against God. The people will respond either positively or negatively, according to the way in which they use their freedom. St. Paul's farewell to the Ephesian elders in Acts 20:26-27 exhibits a similar awareness of his obligation as a prophetic teacher to warn his Christian communities: "Therefore I testify to you this day that I am innocent of the blood of all of you, for I did not shrink from declaring to you the whole counsel of God."

The Lord's Glory Leaves the Temple

In Ezekiel 10 and 11 the prophet, who is still in Babylon, reports to his fellow exiles a vision of the glory of the Lord leaving the temple and the city of Jerusalem. Ezekiel identifies the living creatures from his first vision as cherubim (Ezekiel 10:15-22). He sees the glory of the Lord departing from the temple and standing over the cherubim. Then he sees the cherubim, along with the glory of the Lord, moving away from Jerusalem to the Mount of Olives to the east (11:22).

Other powerful visions of Ezekiel make clear why God's glory left the temple and Jerusalem. Ezekiel 16 is a most vivid parable of Jerusalem as the Lord's unfaithful wife. Unlike most harlots, who receive money for their harlotry, Jerusalem has paid her lovers (see Ezekiel 16:30-34). Her sins surpass even those of her sister cities Samaria to the north and Sodom to the south (see 16:46-58). Yet Jerusalem will be filled with shame when God forgives her all her harlotry (see 16:59-63).

As Jeremiah did (see Jeremiah 31:29-30), Ezekiel also insists that each person will bear responsibility for his or her own sins (see Ezekiel 18). Whereas earlier generations of Israelites may have emphasized how children suffer for the sins of their parents, the focus of both Jeremiah and Ezekiel on the moral responsibility of each person for his or her own behavior will carry over into later apocalyptic emphasis that God will judge both the good and the evil that we have done. Jesus' preaching (see John 9:1-3) continues this motif, and treatments of the final judgment in apocalyptic writings and in Revelation presume this understanding.

But Ezekiel's emphasis on judgment also presumes God's statement to Ezekiel:

> Therefore I will judge you, O house of Israel, every one according to his ways, says the Lord GOD. Repent and turn from all your transgressions, lest iniquity be your ruin. Cast away from you all the transgressions which you have committed against me, and get yourselves a new heart and a new spirit! Why will you die, O house of Israel? For I have no pleasure in the death of any one, says the Lord GOD; so turn, and live.

EZEKIEL 18:30-32

God emphasizes impending judgment so as to urge our repentance, for God does not desire anyone to be lost: "I have no pleasure in the death of any one, says the Lord GOD; so turn, and live" (18:32). Throughout biblical history he has pleaded with self-willed humans to "turn [that is, repent and change your conduct from evil to good] and live."

Pagan Pretensions and Paradise Lost

Ezekiel's oracles against the king of Tyre (who at the time was rebelling against Babylon) utilize imagery from the expulsion from Eden that renders them applicable far beyond their original purpose of criticizing a contemporary ruler. The sin of this pagan king is like the sin of Adam: wanting to "be like God, knowing good and evil" (Genesis 3:5). The prophecy applies other components of the Eden narrative, which by the time of Ezekiel had often been intermingled with traditions about Mount Zion:

> Son of man, say to the prince of Tyre, Thus says the Lord GOD: "Because your heart is proud, and you have said, 'I am a god, I sit in the seat of the gods, in the heart of the seas,' yet you are but a man, and no god, though you consider yourself as wise as a god…you shall die the death of the slain in the heart of the seas…. Will you still say, 'I am a god,' in the presence of those who slay you, though you are but a man, and no god, in the hands of those who wound you?…You were…full of wisdom and perfect in beauty. You were in Eden, the garden of God…. With an anointed guardian cherub I placed you; you were on the holy mountain of God…. You were blameless in your ways from the day you were created, till iniquity was found in you.
>
> EZEKIEL 28:2, 8-9, 12-13, 14, 15

Because the king has fallen into pride and sin, God tells him:

> I cast you as a profane thing from the mountain of God, and the guardian cherub drove you out from the midst of the stones of fire. Your heart was proud because of your beauty; you corrupted your wisdom for the sake of your splendor. I cast you to the ground.
>
> EZEKIEL 28:16b-17a

The echoes of Genesis will find further resonance in apocalyptic verdicts against sins of pride.

Condemnation of the Shepherds

Ezekiel's indictment of the "shepherds of Israel" will play a major role in later prophetic and apocalyptic works, as well as in the teachings of Jesus. Through Ezekiel God strongly condemns the leaders of Israel for providing for themselves rather than caring for their sheep:

> The weak you have not strengthened, the sick you have not healed, the crippled you have not bound up, the strayed you have not brought back, the lost you have not sought, and with force and harshness you have ruled them. So they were scattered, because there was no shepherd; and they became food for all the wild beasts.
>
> EZEKIEL 34:4-5

God himself will oppose these false shepherds and protect his sheep from their greed and mistreatment. God himself will seek out and gather his sheep that have been scattered. "And I will bring them out from the peoples, and gather them from the countries, and will bring them into their own land; and I will feed them on the mountains of Israel, by the fountains, and in all the inhabited places of the country" (Ezekiel 34:13). Rejecting the rulers, God declares, "I myself will be the shepherd of my sheep" (34:15). He himself will provide for them: "I will seek the lost, and I will bring back the strayed, and I will bind up the crippled, and I will strengthen the weak, and the fat and the strong I will watch over; I will feed them in justice" (34:16).

Although the Lord himself says he will shepherd his sheep, Ezekiel also relays God's promise that he will shepherd them through a new David (see Ezekiel 34:23). Under the new and eschatological David, the primeval peace of the Garden of Eden will return to the land: "I will make with them a covenant of peace and banish wild beasts from the land, so that they may dwell securely in the wilderness and sleep in the woods" (34:25).

The trees and the land will be abundantly fruitful, and the people will dwell in security and peace under the protection of their God:

> And they shall know that I, the LORD their God, am with them, and that they, the house of Israel, are my people, says the Lord GOD. And you are my sheep, the sheep of my pasture, and I am your God, says the Lord GOD.
>
> EZEKIEL 34:30-31

Both God's promises—that he himself will shepherd Israel, and that he will do this through a new David—are to be fulfilled when God through his only Son becomes the "good shepherd" and messianic restorer of Israel. Compare John 10 and the ironic fulfillment in Revelation 7:16-17:

> They shall hunger no more, neither thirst any more; the sun shall not strike them, nor any scorching heat. For the Lamb in the midst of the throne will be their shepherd, and he will guide them to springs of living water; and God will wipe away every tear from their eyes.

Oracle of Comfort

Ezekiel 36 has a powerful oracle of comfort for God's people, who have lost hope during their exile. God explains that when they were living in their own land, their sinful behavior so defiled it that God was forced to punish them. He did so by allowing them to be exiled. "But when they came to the nations, wherever they came, they profaned my holy name, in that men said of them, 'These are the people of the LORD, and yet they had to go out of his land'" (36:20). God's people were thus tarnishing his good name by the implication that pagans were drawing from their exile—that

Israel's God was not strong enough among the other gods to protect his own people.

> And I will vindicate the holiness of my great name, which has been profaned among the nations, and which you have profaned among them; and the nations will know that I am the LORD, says the Lord GOD, when through you I vindicate my holiness before their eyes.
>
> EZEKIEL 36:23

Even though the sinful Israelites do not deserve to be forgiven nor brought back to their land, God's good name among the nations is prompting him to rescue and restore his people. Though it may not sound like it, this rationale for God's saving them is good news (even if humiliating to Judah's pride), for it is much more trustworthy than any promise that would depend on the people's own merits.

For the sake of his own name, therefore, God promises that he will gather the exiles from foreign countries to their own land. But what can God do with such a faithless people to prevent their relapsing into the same sins for which they were exiled? God's answer is comparable to his promise to Jeremiah (see Jeremiah 31:31-34). He will cleanse and transform the people's inner selves to make them more responsive to his will:

> I will sprinkle clean water upon you, and you shall be clean from all your uncleannesses, and from all your idols I will cleanse you. A new heart I will give you, and a new spirit I will put within you; and I will take out of your flesh the heart of stone and give you a heart of flesh. And I will put my spirit within you, and cause you to walk in my statutes and be careful to observe my ordinances.
>
> EZEKIEL 36:25-27

With their new heart and God's spirit, the people will be able to remain in their land as God's obedient people (see 36:28).

The "Dry Bones" Prophecy

God assures his disheartened exiles that he can restore them, no matter how hopeless their present situation seems to be. Ezekiel 37 narrates Ezekiel's powerful prophecy of hope to an exiled people who considered their nation to be as dead and without hope as a valley full of dry bones. "And he said to me, 'Son of man, can these bones live?'" (Ezekiel 37:3). God commands Ezekiel to prophesy to the bones:

> Thus says the Lord GOD to these bones: Behold, I will cause breath [spirit] to enter you, and you shall live. And I will lay sinews upon you, and will cause flesh to come upon you, and cover you with skin, and put breath in you, and you shall live; and you shall know that I am the LORD.
>
> EZEKIEL 37:5-6

"So I prophesied as he commanded me, and the breath [spirit] came into them, and they lived, and stood upon their feet, an exceedingly great host" (37:10). God explains to Ezekiel that "these bones are the whole house of Israel" (37:11a).

Israel has been complaining in despair, "Our bones are dried up, and our hope is lost; we are clean cut off" (Ezekiel 37:11b). God assures them:

> Behold, I will open your graves, and raise you from your graves, O my people; and I will bring you home into the land of Israel.... And I will put my Spirit within you, and you shall live, and I will place you in your own land; then you shall know that I, the LORD, have spoken, and I have done it, says the LORD.
>
> EZEKIEL 37:12b, 14

In its original context, God is promising to revive a group of dispirited exiles into a living nation. However, Christians can apply this powerful imagery to the actual physical resurrection of the dead, of which Christ's resurrection will serve as the "first fruits."

In this context of resurrection of the nation, Ezekiel's last prophecy before his oracles about Gog and Magog reasserts God's promise to rule his restored people forever through a new David:

> My servant David shall be king over them; and they shall all [that is, Israelites from both the northern and southern kingdoms] have one shepherd. They shall follow my ordinances and be careful to observe my statutes. They shall dwell in the land where your fathers dwelt that I gave to my servant Jacob; they and their children and their children's children shall dwell there for ever; and David my servant shall be their prince for ever. I will make a covenant of peace with them; it shall be an everlasting covenant with them; and I will bless them and multiply them, and will set my sanctuary in the midst of them for evermore. My dwelling place shall be with them; and I will be their God, and they shall be my people. Then the nations will know that I the LORD sanctify Israel, when my sanctuary is in the midst of them for evermore.
>
> EZEKIEL 37:24-28

This prophecy of everlasting kingship, covenant, and temple will be applied to God's Son, Jesus, Immanuel ("God with us"). This "David" in the end times will assume everlasting rule over God's restored and reunited twelve tribes (see Acts 2:22-36 and Revelation 22:16).

Apocalyptic Battle Against Gog of Magog

In cosmic apocalyptic language, Ezekiel prophesies the defeat in the battle of Gog of Magog. Because the prophecy uses cosmic symbolism and is not merely a straightforward report, and because even today scholars are not certain about the identity of Gog or Magog, this description can and will be reused by later writers to describe the upheavals of the end times. Thus Revelation 20:7-10 prophesies that

Satan will deceive "the nations which are at the four corners of the earth, that is, Gog and Magog, to gather them for battle" (20:8). Gog may relate to a great leader from the past, known to the Greeks as Gyges and to the Assyrians as Gugu. Both Ezekiel and Revelation use the name to portray a future threat, as one might refer to "a new Hitler."[2]

Ezekiel mentions that many nations are allied with Gog against Israel (see Ezekiel 38:5-8). God addresses Gog, their leader:

> You will come up against my people Israel, like a cloud
> covering the land. In the latter days I will bring you against
> my land, that the nations may know me, when through
> you, O Gog, I vindicate my holiness before their eyes.
>
> EZEKIEL 38:16

Using the forces of nature, God himself will fight for Israel against the powerful enemies, and finally he "will rain upon [Gog] and his hordes and the many peoples that are with him, torrential rains and hailstones, fire and brimstone" (38:22b). After this battle there will be enough wood in the captured weapons of Gog's defeated forces for the Israelites to burn for fuel for seven years. There will be so many corpses from Gog's army that it will take the Israelites seven months to bury them all and to cleanse their land from pollution (see 39:9-16).

The Restored Temple and Land

Ezekiel hopes that the exile will end by the fiftieth year, the year of Jubilee (its duration was actually closer to Jeremiah's seventy years). At the halfway mark, "in the twenty-fifth year of our exile" (Ezekiel 40:1), he receives a vision of the restored temple of the end times. Ezekiel 40–42 narrates this vision with multiple measurements made, on the prophet's behalf, by "a man, whose appearance was like bronze, with a line of flax and a measuring reed in his hand" (40:3).

This vision of the angelic measurer builds upon the promise in Ezekiel 37:26-28 that God would restore his sanctuary among his people. In Revelation, however, this promise has undergone a "transfiguration." The promise that God will be personally present among his people persists, but in Revelation God himself will be their temple: "And I saw no temple in the city, for its temple is the Lord God the Almighty and the Lamb" (Revelation 21:22). The New Testament has definitively and repeatedly reinterpreted Jewish prophetic hopes of a restored temple, such as those in Ezekiel, and has transferred the promised divine presence among his people to a presence in Christ (for example, "The Word became flesh and dwelt among us," in John 1:14 and, "He spoke of the temple of his body," in John 2:21), or simply to God himself (see Revelation 21:22). Thus in Revelation the angel's measurements apply not to a new temple but to the New Jerusalem itself come down from heaven (Revelation 21:2):

> And he who talked to me had a measuring rod of gold to measure the city and its gates and walls. The city lies foursquare, its length the same as its breadth; and he measured the city with his rod, twelve thousand stadia; its length and breadth and height are equal. He also measured its wall, a hundred and forty-four cubits by a man's measure, that is, an angel's.
>
> REVELATION 21:15-17

In view of the prophecy in Ezekiel 10–11 that God's glory will depart from the temple toward the east, Ezekiel 43 narrates his vision of the return of God's glory from the east to the temple, which it fills (see Ezekiel 43:1-5). God promises Ezekiel that he will dwell with his people in this temple forever and that Israel shall no longer defile God's holy name (see 43:7-9). The entire top of Mount Zion shall be holy, not only the temple (see 43:10-12).

As we have noted, this expectation about the holiness of Zion will reappear in Revelation but in an evolved form. Since in Revelation all of Zion will be the holy sanctuary of God's presence, nothing unclean can enter it. For the New Jerusalem is "the holy city" from heaven, adorned as a bride (Revelation 21:2). It has no temple, "for its temple is the Lord God the Almighty and the Lamb" (21:22). "Nothing unclean shall enter it, nor any one who practices abomination or falsehood, but only those who are written in the Lamb's book of life" (21:27).

In his visions during Judah's exile and after the destruction of Solomon's temple, the prophet Ezekiel is given the dimensions of the new altar and instructions on how animals are to be sacrificed, how blood is to be applied to the altar, and how the altar is to be purified and consecrated (see Ezekiel 43:13-27). The profanation of the old temple and abuses by the Levites will no longer be tolerated, but the faithful Zadokite priests shall enter the sanctuary and minister before God with holy garments of linen (see 44:15-19). These priests are to "have no inheritance; I am their inheritance" (44:28). They shall eat of the first fruits and other temple offerings by the other tribes (see 44:29-31).

When the land is allotted after the return from exile, a portion shall become a holy district for the Lord, divided between the priests and Levites (see Ezekiel 45:1-5). The princes shall have their own land and shall no more oppress the people in their tribal lands and possessions. They are to use just weights and balances and make offerings on their own behalf and that of the people (see 45:7-25).

This vision and prophecy are so idealistic that by comparison the actual second temple that was built after the exile became a disappointment to the people. Even today some subdivisions of Judaism—and, more surprisingly, even some Christians—are still waiting for these prophecies of Ezekiel to be fulfilled through a new physical temple to be built on the site of former temples in Jerusalem. These Christians believe that God's promises and work with Judaism and the Church are two wholly unrelated and parallel dispensations (which is why they are sometimes called "Dispensationalists").[3]

However, the New Testament (specifically, John, Hebrews, and Revelation) makes quite clear that these prophecies of a new temple and Jerusalem (like all prophecies of the Old Testament, even idealized ones) have their fulfillment in Jesus, who is himself the new temple:

> "Destroy this temple, and in three days I will raise it up." The Jews then said, "It has taken forty-six years to build this temple, and will you raise it up in three days?" But he spoke of the temple of his body. When therefore he was raised from the dead, his disciples remembered that he had said this; and they believed the scripture and the word which Jesus had spoken.
>
> JOHN 2:19-22

The Sacred River from the Temple

Ezekiel's powerful vision of the sacred river flowing from the temple toward the east utilizes symbols that will reappear in other end times writings, including Revelation. As it flows to the east the water becomes deeper, and when it enters the Dead Sea it makes those stagnant waters fresh. Thus, in what was formerly the Dead Sea, there will be swarms of living creatures. Fishermen will fish its rejuvenated waters. This prophetic image is especially forceful to me because I personally experienced how deadly the Dead Sea is. I saw how minnows swimming into it died the instant they hit the sea's brackish waters.

On the banks of this river the trees will bear fresh fruit every month, and their leaves will be for healing (see Ezekiel 47:12). Compare this with an even more idealized vision in Revelation 22:1-2, which makes reference to the

Garden of Eden and to the Tree of Life within it. Whereas in Ezekiel the river flows from the temple, in Revelation it flows from the throne of God and of the Lamb, who take the place of the temple:

> Then he showed me the river of the water of life, bright as crystal, flowing from the throne of God and of the Lamb through the middle of the street of the city; also, on either side of the river, the tree of life with its twelve kinds of fruit, yielding its fruit each month; and the leaves of the tree were for the healing of the nations.

In the rest of Ezekiel's vision, God establishes the boundaries within the Holy Land for all twelve restored tribes. In effect, this becomes a vision of the promised restoration of Israel in the end times. For even at the later times of Jesus and of the New Testament writers, the "ten lost tribes" of the northern kingdom of Israel have not been returned to the Holy Land, from which Assyria had scattered them all over the known world eight centuries earlier. In contrast, Cyrus has allowed the two tribes of the southern kingdom of Judah to return to the Holy Land after their exile in Babylon (see Isaiah 44:28–45:1).

Thus when New Testament writers refer to the twelve tribes as a present or future reality, they are referring not to any currently existing twelve tribes but to an idealized twelve tribes to be restored in the end times. Along these lines, the Letter of James begins, "James, a servant of God and of the Lord Jesus Christ, To the twelve tribes in the Dispersion: Greeting" (James 1:1). Compare a similar image in 1 Peter: "Peter, an apostle of Jesus Christ. To the exiles of the Dispersion in Pontus, Galatia, Cappadocia, Asia, and Bithynia, chosen and destined by God the Father and sanctified by the Spirit for obedience to Jesus Christ and for sprinkling with his blood" (1 Peter 1:1-2). Both writers are addressing communities of Christians. This set of visions in

Ezekiel has its concluding climax in a vision of the New Jerusalem, with its twelve gates named after the twelve tribes of Israel (see Ezekiel 48:30-35).

The Transition from Prophetic to Apocalyptic in Daniel

In the descriptions of Ezekiel's visions, the prophetic imagery and symbolism have already begun to border on the bizarre and fantastic. The tendency toward ever more extravagant symbolism comes to its full development in the new type of biblical writings called apocalyptic (Greek for "revelation"). The Book of Daniel is the first major apocalyptic work in Scripture.

This kind of writing first emerged after it began to appear that classical prophecy had ceased. Unlike most prophetic oracles and writings, apocalyptic works tended to express their revelations in cryptic and mysterious language and images. Among later apocalyptic writings will be Revelation in the New Testament.

The apocalyptic aura of mystery is heightened by the fact that most apocalypses portray their messages as originating from some hero of the ancient past and as being "sealed" to be opened in some future age. For example, there are apocalypses attributed to such ancient ancestors as Enoch, Ezra, Baruch, Abraham, Elijah, and even Adam. Revelation is an exception to this Jewish practice. There the author identifies himself not only as the visionary but also as a contemporary Christian prophet. He reveals his true name, John, as well as the actual circumstances of his revelations, as he was suffering exile on the island of Patmos for his witness to his faith in Jesus (see Revelation 1:9-11).

The first six chapters of the Book of Daniel contain older stories about a wise man, Daniel, from an earlier era. The stories are set during the Babylonian exile in the sixth century B.C. (see Ezekiel 14:14; 28:3), whereas Daniel 7 through 12 present visions received during the later Hellenistic period of writing (second century B.C.). As most apocalypses did, the visions in Daniel are presented as if they were received centuries earlier by a famous seer— namely, the hero of Daniel 1–6. This follows the Jewish practice of writing under the names of ancient authors. Internal historical references in the visions prompt scholars to ascribe these visions quite narrowly to a Jewish seer suffering under the persecution of the later Greek emperor, Antiochus IV Epiphanes, in 167-164 B.C., the same persecution that 1 and 2 Maccabees describe.

Daniel's Interpretation of King Nebuchadnezzar's Dream

The older account of Daniel interpreting King Nebuchadnezzar's dream in Daniel 2 provides a helpful introduction to the visions from the Hellenistic age in Daniel 7 through 12. After the king demands that his wise men not only interpret his vision but first tell him what the vision is, Daniel says to him:

> No wise men, enchanters, magicians, or astrologers can show to the king the mystery which the king has asked, but there is a God in heaven who reveals mysteries, and he has made known to King Nebuchadnezzar what will be in the latter days.
>
> DANIEL 2:27-28

This belief in God's ability to reveal and interpret mysteries through chosen visionaries is foundational for apocalyptic and end times writings.

Daniel interprets the dream to refer to the reign of Nebuchadnezzar and to kingdoms that will follow it, each kingdom being somewhat less powerful than the previous one. Finally in "the latter days" God himself will establish a kingdom that will never end:

> And in the days of those kings the God of heaven will set up a kingdom which shall never be destroyed, nor shall its sovereignty be left to another people. It shall break in pieces all these kingdoms and bring them to an end, and it shall stand for ever; just as you saw that a stone was cut from a mountain by no human hand, and that it broke in pieces the iron, the bronze, the clay, the silver, and the gold. A great God has made known to the king what shall be hereafter. The dream is certain, and its interpretation sure.
>
> DANIEL 2:44-45

The king's reaction is to praise Daniel's God: "Truly, your God is God of gods and Lord of kings, and a revealer of mysteries, for you have been able to reveal this mystery" (2:47). The relationship between God's revealed mysteries, Daniel, and the king provide the narrative setting for the apocalyptic visions that the author of the Book of Daniel will recount, beginning in Daniel 7.

Apocalyptic Visions of Daniel 7

Daniel's "vision by night" (that is, his dream) is of four beasts arising from the great sea. The first three are respectively like a lion with eagle's wings, like a bear, and like a four-headed leopard with wings (see Daniel 7:3-6).

> After this I saw in the night visions, and behold, a fourth beast, terrible and dreadful and exceedingly strong; and it had great iron teeth; it devoured and broke in pieces, and stamped the residue with its feet. It was different from all the beasts that were before it; and it had ten horns. I considered the horns, and behold, there came up among them another horn, a little one, before which three of the first horns were plucked up by the roots; and behold, in this horn were eyes like the eyes of a man, and a mouth speaking great things.
>
> DANIEL 7:7-8

The four beasts from the sea represent four successive empires: the Babylonians, the Medes, the Persians, and the Greeks. These four correspond to the four successive empires from the Babylonian empire, at the time of the stories in Daniel 1 through 6, to the Greek or Seleucid empire at the time of the vision in Daniel 7. The fourth of these, the Hellenistic empire founded by the conquests of Alexander the Great, was the fiercest.

The "little horn with the big mouth" represents the arrogant Greek Emperor Antiochus IV Epiphanes, the tenth emperor in the line begun by Alexander the Great. Antiochus was the ruler who persecuted the Jews and profaned their temple. Of course, because the empires are portrayed symbolically as beasts, later prophets and apocalyptic seers can reinterpret the symbolism and apply these beasts to different historical nations, as the Book of Revelation will do in applying the fourth beast to Rome.[4]

A vision of the heavenly throne room with God sitting in judgment is heaven's response to this fierce empire and arrogant emperor.

> As I looked, thrones were placed and one that was ancient of days took his seat; his raiment was white as snow, and the hair of his head like pure wool; his throne was fiery flames, its wheels were burning fire. A stream of fire issued and came forth from before him; a thousand thousands served him, and ten thousand times ten thousand stood before him; the court sat in judgment, and the books were opened.
>
> DANIEL 7:9-10

The similarities of this vision in Daniel to the throne vision in Ezekiel (see Ezekiel 1:26-28) are immediately conspicuous (compare also the throne vision in Isaiah 6). In both visions the divine throne is associated with flames and wheels, and a heavenly court surrounds it to praise and serve God. These and other details will also recur in John's vision of God on his throne in Revelation 4.

It seems apparent that each prophet or seer is attempting to narrate and describe his personal vision of God on his throne. Each prophet experiences his vision as awe-inspiring, terrifying, and ultimately beyond description. How can one describe an indescribable experience of God? One naturally consults or recalls descriptions of similar visions in earlier prophets and biblical books. From those analogous visions the visionary finds language and symbolism to approximate and express his own vision. Thus Ezekiel consults a comparable vision in Isaiah for images with which to describe his slightly different personal vision of God enthroned; Daniel in the same way borrows from a vision in Ezekiel that has elements in common with what he saw; and John on Patmos will benefit from visions of them all in describing his own comparable vision.

The expression "ancient of days" and the white clothing and hair represent God's eternity and wisdom. The fiery flames in his throne reveal God's purifying holiness. (Compare the burning coal that purifies Isaiah's lips in Isaiah 6.) The myriads of heavenly creatures stand ready as the heavenly court is convened and the books of accusations, good and bad deeds, and divine judgments are opened in order to judge the four nations symbolized by the four beasts.

The first to be judged is the fourth beast and the little horn with the big mouth speaking arrogantly (Daniel 7:11). This beast is judged the most harshly: It is slain and its body burnt. The nation it represents (the Greek empire) is to be utterly destroyed. The other three nation-beasts lose their dominion but are allowed to survive as nations (7:12).

One Like a Son of Man

The climax of this vision is the coming of "one like a son of man" before the Ancient of Days. "I saw in the night visions, and behold, with the clouds of heaven there came one like a son of man, and he came to the Ancient of Days and was presented before him" (Daniel 7:13). The New Testament will quote and allude to this vision many times, beginning with the sayings of Jesus and culminating in Revelation. After the judgment of the four nation-beasts, the figure of "one like a son of man" approaches God on the clouds. He appears before the throne for the implementation of God's judgment and sentence.

In most apocalyptic visions, animals tend to symbolize human figures and nations (as in the four beasts for the four human nations), whereas human forms tend to represent angelic figures. Thus this figure of the "one like a son of man" may well have originally symbolized an angelic figure. In Daniel, the angel who guards and guides Israel is Michael (see Daniel 12:1: "At that time shall arise Michael, the great prince who has charge of your people"; see 10:21). In biblical symbolism, it is also common for the leader of a people to stand for the people he leads: Thus the term Israel represents both the ancestor and the nation named after him.

In this original context, the "one like a son of man" could represent both the archangel Michael and the people Israel whom he protects. However, in Scripture it is more common for God to grant earthly dominion to humans than to angels. So even if the "one like a son of man" reminded its first readers of the archangel Michael, the expression clearly implies the people Israel, whom Michael represents both on the heavenly battlefield and in the heavenly court. As in the beginning God gave dominion over the whole world to Adam, he will give it to the people Israel in the end times. The linkage between the "one like a son of man" and the people Israel is confirmed in the explanation of the vision in Daniel 7:18: "But the saints of the Most High shall receive the kingdom, and possess the kingdom for ever, for ever and ever" (see 7:27).

There is a widespread, even if not fully conscious,

propensity among contemporary scholars to consider the christological titles of Messiah and Son of Man as unrelated. However, a closer look at the role of "one like a son of man" in Daniel 7 reveals that it corresponds almost completely to the traditional role of the Messiah, although without the latter's claim to Davidic kingship:

> And to him was given dominion and glory and kingdom, that all peoples, nations, and languages should serve him; his dominion is an everlasting dominion, which shall not pass away, and his kingdom one that shall not be destroyed.
>
> DANIEL 7:14

Although Daniel 7:18 puts the original focus of this vision on the unending rule of the people of Israel over all the nations in the end times, several New Testament authors, and probably Jesus himself, saw in this "one like a son of man" an image of the human messianic ruler of Israel in the end times. For nation and ruler are often interchangeable in biblical symbolism. From the concept of a messianic ruler in the end times to a foreshadowing and prophecy of Jesus the risen Messiah himself is a simple logical step.

Thus, for Christian readers, after Jesus' resurrection as Messiah, he will represent the people Israel in the final days (see Acts 2:36). Those final days begin with the outpouring of the Holy Spirit by the risen Christ (see the Joel quotation in Acts 2:16-21). To the risen Messiah, Jesus, will be given "dominion and glory and kingdom" over all "peoples, nations, and languages." His dominion will last forever; it will never pass away or be destroyed.

Daniel 9: Seventy Weeks of Years
Chapter 9 of Daniel presents calculations of future periods of time that have played a prominent role in end time scenarios that purport to be based on biblical prophecies. These

reflections and scenarios begin within the Book of Daniel itself, as Daniel reflects on Jeremiah's prophecy of the length of time that Jerusalem's punishment will endure:

> In the first year of his reign, I, Daniel, perceived in the books the number of years which, according to the word of the LORD to Jeremiah the prophet, must pass before the end of the desolations of Jerusalem, namely, seventy years.
>
> DANIEL 9:2, referring to JEREMIAH 25:11;29:10

Jeremiah's seventy years are typical biblical round numbers expressing, for example, a normal human lifetime, rather than the precise numbers such as twenty-eight or forty-one that the Books of Kings tell us various kings reigned.[5] The primary point of Jeremiah's prophecy toward the beginning of the exilic period was to warn his fellow exiles that their deportation was going to last a long time, an entire lifetime. As a matter of fact, the exilic period—from the destruction of the temple to the return to Jerusalem—did last approximately seventy years. However, after their return to Jerusalem, the Jews remained subject to foreign powers—Persian, Greek, and eventually Roman. Many Jews continued to regard and to refer to this foreign domination as an extension of the exile proper. According to the principle of sevenfold punishment in Leviticus 26, Jewish interpreters therefore multiplied Jeremiah's seventy years times seven to arrive at roughly 490 years, which brought the time reckoning much closer to their own times in the second century B.C. Four hundred ninety years also became the standard for calculating periods in salvation history.[6]

Scholars have wisely cautioned against approaches that obsessively treat the 490 years as strict chronological information and that as a result either fault or vindicate Daniel's figures.[7] This attempt to calculate strict chronological time spans seems common to most contemporary arguments about the end times or "the rapture" and even to some

Catholic responses to fundamentalist calculations about the rapture and end times.[8] Stylized schemes of history correspond much more closely to the prevalent symbolic and metaphorical uses that the Bible makes of cosmology, genealogy, and arithmology (for example, seven as a perfect number, 666 as the ultimate in imperfection).[9]

Some biblical numbers seem to combine a factual chronological basis with later symbolic meanings. Thus, although the three and a half years in Daniel 7:25 and elsewhere are half of the symbolic number seven, they also correspond approximately to the actual amount of time between the profanation of the temple by the Greek emperor Antiochus and its reconsecration (from 167 to 164 B.C.). Daniel 7:25 reads:

> [Antiochus] shall speak words against the Most High, and shall wear out the saints of the Most High, and shall think to change the times and the law; and they shall be given into his hand for a time, two times, and half a time.

Revelation will repeatedly reapply or appeal to these same three and a half years (12:4)—or forty-two months (13:5) or 1,260 days (11:3)—as almost a standard symbolic number for the time of intense persecution. Thus a close approximation of the historical time during which the temple actually suffered profanation, that is, three and a half years, becomes a standard biblical symbolic duration of extreme persecution.

The explanation by Gabriel begins in Daniel 9:24 with the 490-year prophecy, but its wording is symbolic enough to transcend its probably original reference to the desolation and restoration of the temple under the persecution of the Greek emperor Antiochus.

> Seventy weeks of years are decreed concerning your people and your holy city, to finish the transgression, to put an end to sin, and to atone for iniquity, to bring in

> everlasting righteousness, to seal both vision and
> prophet, and to anoint a most holy place.
>
> DANIEL 9:24

This wording can be applied to the original outrage of
Antiochus' profanation of the temple and to its purification
about three and a half years later. But promises in this verse,
such as "to put an end to sin" and "to bring in everlasting
righteousness," suggest far more universal evils than those
experienced by the Maccabees at the time of Daniel 7–12, as
well as a fulfillment that is conceivable only in the end times.
Daniel 9:27 seems to apply directly to circumstances relating
to Emperor Antiochus and the Maccabees:

> And he shall make a strong covenant with many for one
> week; and for half of the week he shall cause sacrifice and
> offering to cease; and upon the wing of abominations
> shall come one who makes desolate, until the decreed
> end is poured out on the desolator.

Antiochus had made agreements with Hellenizing Jews that
Jewish culture and religion would conform more closely to
their Hellenistic Greek milieu.

Halfway through this period the emperor put an end to
temple sacrifices and profaned the temple with the "abomination that makes desolate" (Daniel 11:31; 12:11; see 1
Maccabees 1:54; 6:7). However, merely three and a half
years after he profaned the temple, the emperor Antiochus
died an ignominious death: "So the murderer and blasphe-
mer, having endured the most intense suffering, such as he
had inflicted on others, came to the end of his life by a most
pitiable fate, among the mountains in a strange land"
(2 Maccabees 9:28).

Mark 13:14 makes a mysterious reference to a future
abomination that will be similar to the abomination in
Daniel: "But when you see the desolating sacrilege set up

where it ought not to be (let the reader understand), then let those who are in Judea flee to the mountains." Matthew's version of this prophecy of Jesus makes explicit its reference to Daniel: "So when you see the desolating sacrilege spoken of by the prophet Daniel, standing in the holy place (let the reader understand), then let those who are in Judea flee to the mountains" (Matthew 24:15-16).

As is common in biblical prophecy in times of extreme duress, promises often have an almost messianic and eschatological tone of ideal renewal that far exceeds their historical fulfillment. Thus, not only will the transgression (sacrilege to the temple) be brought to an end, but the prophecy also makes idyllic promises "to put an end to sin, and to atone for iniquity, to bring in everlasting righteousness," which are more properly expectations for the end times. The promise "to seal both vision and prophet, and to anoint a most holy place" can indeed apply to the fulfillment of Jeremiah's prophecy in the restoration of the temple profaned by Antiochus but is certainly not exhausted by that event.

The New Testament, including sayings of Jesus, sees a more comprehensive fulfillment of this prophecy in the destruction of the second temple in A.D. 70 and in the restoration of "this temple" in the resurrected body of the Messiah. Compare John 2:19-21:

> Jesus answered them, "Destroy this temple, and in three days I will raise it up." The Jews then said, "It has taken forty-six years to build this temple, and will you raise it up in three days?" But he spoke of the temple of his body.

Martyrs and the Resurrection

The visions in Daniel 11–12 portray the rise of Antiochus IV Epiphanes and his persecution of the Jews and profanation of their temple. "Forces from him shall appear and profane the temple and fortress, and shall take away the continual burnt offering. And they shall set up the abomination that makes desolate" (Daniel 11:31). His persecution will prevail, and he will "exalt himself and magnify himself above every god, and shall speak astonishing things against the God of gods" (11:36). However, at the time that he seems unstoppable, at the height of his power, this blaspheming emperor "shall come to his end, with none to help him" (11:45b).

Israel's guardian angel Michael shall come to the people's rescue: "At that time shall arise Michael, the great prince who has charge of your people.... At that time your people shall be delivered, every one whose name shall be found written in the book" (Daniel 12:1). Not only will the living be rescued, but Daniel also gives the clearest early expression in Scripture of a prophecy that the dead shall be raised: "And many of those who sleep in the dust of the earth shall awake, some to everlasting life, and some to shame and everlasting contempt" (12:2). This is a very early prophecy that there shall be a double resurrection—a resurrection to everlasting life and a resurrection for endless punishment.

An analogous belief that Jews who were martyred in this same Greek persecution will be resurrected from the dead appears in 2 Maccabees, particularly in the account of the martyrdom of the seven brothers (2 Maccabees 7). Before dying the second brother says to the emperor, "You accursed wretch, you dismiss us from this present life, but the King of the universe will raise us up to an everlasting renewal of life, because we have died for his laws" (7:9). At the point of death the fourth brother says, "One cannot but choose to die at the hands of men and to cherish the hope that God gives of being raised again by him. But for you there will be no resurrection to life!" (7:14). The mother exhorts her sons:

> Therefore the Creator of the world, who shaped the
> beginning of man and devised the origin of all things, will

> in his mercy give life and breath back to you again, since
> you now forget yourselves for the sake of his laws.
>
> 2 MACCABEES 7:23

Despite the intense Greek cultural prejudice against the value of the human body and therefore resistance to any belief that human bodies will be resurrected, several writings concerning this period arrive at an explicit hope for and belief in resurrection of the dead. Otherwise, there seemed no justice for dedicated Jews who were willing to be tortured to death by Greek rulers precisely because of their faith in and fidelity to God.

However, the original context of Daniel 12 could also imply a symbolic sense of resurrection as political rescue and vindication from the persecuting tyrant "at that time" (Daniel 12:1). Even if there is this symbolic sense, the seer's vocabulary and language clearly transcend the kinds of double-edged earthly vindication and punishment prayed for in the psalms. Whatever mixture of contemporary politics with the eschatological future may be part of the original experience of this vision, Catholic readers today believe that God as ultimate author of Scripture also used these expressions to point toward a literal resurrection of those who had died. Some were to be raised to "everlasting life," which can only mean heaven, and others "for endless punishment," which only occurs in hell.

Daniel's imagery contains a confusing intermingling of times, between Michael's rescue from the persecuting emperor at the time of the seer and a double-edged resurrection of the dead, which later biblical Jewish and Christian authors have come to expect only at the end of history. Yet the parallel testimony in 2 Maccabees, which was written concerning the same persecution under the same emperor, supports the judgment that Daniel refers to Jewish belief in actual resurrection. Second Maccabees exhibits a Jewish belief, contemporary with Daniel 7–12, that those martyrs who died for their Jewish faith would be raised from the dead. This is significant evidence for seeing Daniel 12:2 as also containing some reference to a literal resurrection. John of Revelation will later emphasize the end time more explicitly than Daniel, when he applies this notion from Daniel of a double resurrection to endless life or punishment at the final judgment.

Conclusion

After the human race decided not to do things God's way but tried themselves to be as God, human history became a constant tug-of-war between God and humans. God continued to invite humans, as images of God, to be his adopted and beloved daughters and sons. Humans continued to rebel against the limits on their freedom that this invitation implied. God proceeded with his plan to salvage our future by preparing a people into which he could eventually send his Son to save us. However, this people too kept rebelling against God and turning to other gods and wanting to control their own destiny.

God's strongest biblical response to this ongoing rebellion is the warnings and corrections in the prophets. We have looked at the main prophetic books of Isaiah, Jeremiah, Ezekiel, and Daniel. In all of them we see escalating warnings and ever more dire prophecies and threats in increasingly more graphic and symbolic language. In this symbolic language the problems and politics of the time of the prophet are expressed in ever more idealized images that realistically must await the end times for their complete fulfillment. Many of the images and prophesied scenarios of these prophets and of the transitional Book of Daniel will become standard symbols for prophecies and apocalyptic visions of the end times in the New Testament, both in the eschatological sayings of Jesus and in the Book of Revelation.

Notes:

1. See the synthetic treatment of Jewish biblical religion in Jon D. Levenson, *Sinai and Zion: An Entry into the Jewish Bible* (New York: HarperCollins [HarperSanFrancisco], 1985).

2. Leslie C. Allen, "Ezekiel 20-48" in *Word Biblical Commentary*, 29 (Dallas: Word, 1990), 204-5.

3. See the interview with Carl Olson, "Was Jesus a Failure?" in *The Catholic World Report* 13, no. 8 (August/September 2003), 44-52: "A fundamentalist convert to Catholicism examines prophecies about the rapture and the end times, and shows how a very popular form of Protestant thought springs from theological premises that actually downplay the role of Christ."

4. Failure to distinguish Revelation's reinterpretation of Daniel's fourth beast (the Greek empire) from the Roman empire, the "evil empire" current at the time of Revelation, is one problem I have with the approach of David B. Currie, *Rapture: The End Times Error That Leaves the Bible Behind* (Manchester, N.H.: Sophia, 2003).

5. John E. Goldingay, "Daniel" in *Word Biblical Commentary*, 30 (Dallas: Word, 1989), 258 on Daniel 9:24.

6. Goldingay, 258.

7. Goldingay, 257.

8. This fundamental methodological problem is one of my most serious reservations about Currie.

9. Goldingay, 257.

chapter three

Jesus' Apocalyptic Message:
Matthew 24–25 and Luke 21

The previous chapters situated questions about the end times within the biblical context of Creation and the Fall, relying foundationally on Genesis 1–3. For in describing the final days, the Book of Revelation, as have most apocalyptic works, has made heavy use of images from Creation and primeval times. Revelation has also relied heavily on biblical symbols and images found in the messages of the prophets, who kept trying to call God's people back from their sins to avoid the punishment (often referred to as God's "wrath") that their sins deserved. To provide language and symbolism needed for understanding Revelation, the second chapter brought to the fore these prophetic warnings with their sometimes ominous imagery.

Both chapters took a canonical perspective that was grounded in the presumption that God's revelation throughout Scripture has an underlying unity. Interpreting Genesis 1–3 with the help of later Old Testament and New Testament texts, especially the prologue of John's Gospel, the first chapter highlighted some links between Revelation and Genesis:

- In the beginning God created everything (out of nothing) simply by his word.

- Although one hears very little about Creation in today's homilies and religious education, it truly is the foundation of a biblical worldview and theology.

■ Creation implies an absolute difference between God
the Creator and everything and everyone else, including humans, who are created by God and utterly
dependent on him for their very existence.

The prologue of John further revealed that the command or
word by which God created everything (for example, in
Genesis 1:3, "Let there be light") was actually personal—the
Word, who is the Son of God and who is himself God (John
1:1-3). That humans might be the crown and pinnacle of
God's creation, God "created man in his own image, in the
image of God he created him; male and female he created
them" (Genesis 1:27). Humans, however, were not satisfied
with being in God's image and exercising authority on God's
behalf over the rest of material creation. They tried themselves to "be like God, knowing good and evil" (Genesis
3:5). They "grasped" at "equality with God" (see Philippians
2:6) by disobeying his command, which had placed limits
on their autonomy.

Such a flagrant affront to the Creator was beyond the
ability of human creatures to repair. They had forfeited
God's offer of love and adoption as his sons and daughters
and become hopelessly alienated from God, from one
another, and from all other creatures. The Old Testament
substantiates the rapid proliferation of human corruption
and alienation from God. For example, Genesis 6:5 states,
"The LORD saw that the wickedness of man was great in the
earth, and that every imagination of the thoughts of his
heart was only evil continually." Without God's saving
intervention on their behalf, humans were doomed to eternal separation from God, to hell.

Redemption
We have seen how John's Gospel announces the good news of
God's response to this universal human plight. The creating

Word, the Son of God, "became flesh and dwelt among us" (John 1:14). The *Spiritual Exercises* of St. Ignatius Loyola imagine the Trinitarian God observing the human tragedy and agreeing to send the Son to rescue us:

> The first Prelude is to bring up the narrative of the thing which I have to contemplate. Here, it is how the Three Divine Persons looked at all the plain or circuit of all the world, full of men, and how, seeing that all were going down to Hell, it is determined in Their Eternity that the Second Person shall become man to save the human race.[1]

The entrance of the Son of God into our "flesh," thus sharing in our condition, created a new era in human history. "In the beginning," God delegated his rule and dominion over the earth to man as his image and representative. After humans rejected God's authority over them in Genesis 3, nature in turn rebelled against man, so that instead of bearing fruit it would bear "thorns and thistles." Only by toil, by struggling with recalcitrant nature, would man earn his bread "by the sweat of his brow" (see Genesis 3:17-19).

Victory over Satan

Several books of the Old and New Testaments express the realization that the dominion and rule over the world, which humans forfeited, was seized by Satan and his rebellious angels. It is as if God allowed this satanic domination over most of the earth but separated from it Abraham, through whom he would form a personal people and eventually a kingdom for himself to rule. God's shepherding of his Old Testament people, through both kings and prophets, was to prepare for his eventually reclaiming "in the final days" rule over all the earth in the kingdom of God.

From the beginning God intended his choice of Abraham and his descendants to be a blessing for all the nations. In Genesis 12:3 God tells Abraham, "By you all the families of the earth shall be blessed."[2] Further, in the Hebrew, as interpreted by its Greek and Latin translations, God promises Abraham, after he demonstrated his willingness to sacrifice his only son, "And by your seed shall all the nations of the earth be blessed" (Genesis 22:18).[3] Christians read the collective term seed (or offspring) as a singular term for Abraham's messianic descendant. Thus St. Paul argues, "Now the promises were made to Abraham and to his offspring. It does not say, 'And to offsprings,' referring to many; but, referring to one, 'And to your offspring,' which is Christ" (Galatians 3:16).

The prevailing view in New Testament times was that Satan was exercising widespread control over the earth and many of its inhabitants, with the possible exception of this chosen people. That provides the plausibility, for example, of Satan's claim of dominion in his efforts to tempt Jesus:

> And the devil took him up, and showed him all the kingdoms of the world in a moment of time, and said to him, "To you I will give all this authority and their glory; *for it has been delivered to me, and I give it to whom I will.* If you, then, will worship me, it shall all be yours.'"
>
> LUKE 4:5-7, emphasis added

Similarly, Revelation 12–13 portrays the dragon, identified with Satan, assigning his authority to the beast (in its original reference, clearly the Roman Empire).

Abraham's promised seed, Jesus (see Luke 1:54-55) preached that the "kingdom (reign or rule) of God" was near. Not much longer would Satan maintain the oppressive control over the world that he had held all those centuries. In his many exorcisms, Jesus confirmed the beginning of this overthrow of Satan's domination. Thus Luke quotes Jesus: "But if it is by the finger of God that I cast out demons, then the kingdom of God has come upon you" (Luke 11:20).

Although John's Gospel does not mention individual exorcisms, it makes an even more powerful claim. John's Gospel portrays Jesus' death on the cross as a kind of cosmic exorcism of Satan from his stranglehold over the world. As Jesus contemplates his impending passion, he proclaims, "Now is the judgment of this world, *now shall the ruler of this world be cast out*; and I, when I am lifted up from the earth, will draw all men to myself" (John 12:31-32, emphasis added; see John 14:30: "For the ruler of this world is coming. He has no power over me").

A similar kind of cosmic exorcism through the cross will appear also in Revelation:

> *And the great dragon was thrown down, that ancient serpent, who is called the Devil and Satan, the deceiver of the whole world*—he was thrown down to the earth, and his angels were thrown down with him. And I heard a loud voice in heaven, saying, "Now the salvation and the power and the *kingdom of our God and the authority of his Christ have come*, for the accuser of our brethren has been thrown down, who accuses them day and night before our God. And *they have conquered him by the blood of the Lamb* and by the word of their testimony, for they loved not their lives even unto death."
>
> REVELATION 12:9-11, emphasis added

The prominence here of Jesus' overturning Satan's rule helps explain why the early Church did not continue to emphasize the coming of the kingdom or rule of God, as Jesus himself did in his public ministry. Whereas Jesus accentuated the coming kingdom of God, the early Church emphasized Christology—that is, who Christ is. For through the Word or Son of God made flesh and glorified after the cross, the Church saw the reign of God being implemented by the Holy Spirit, whom Jesus sent or whom God sent in Jesus' name: "Being therefore exalted at the right hand of

God, and having received from the Father the promise of the Holy Spirit, he has poured out this which you see and hear" (Acts 2:33); "But the Counselor, the Holy Spirit, whom the Father will send in my name..." (John 14:26).

Victory Over Sin

A related emphasis in the New Testament and early Church responded to the overcoming of the primeval temptation and sin of trying to "be like God" (Genesis 3:5). This was the theme of divinization through Christ. St. Athanasius sums up an exceptionally widespread patristic theme (from Irenaeus, to Augustine, to Athanasius, and beyond) that has become a centerpiece of the theology of the Eastern Churches: "The Son of God became man so that man could become God."[4] What Adam had ruined, Jesus as second Adam restored. "Then as one man's trespass led to condemnation for all men, so one man's act of righteousness leads to acquittal and life for all men. For as by one man's disobedience many were made sinners, so by one man's obedience many will be made righteous" (Romans 5:18-19, see 5:12-21).

St. Paul's Letter to the Philippians spells out the disposition by which the new Adam reversed the rebellious disobedience of the first Adam, who had striven to "be like God, knowing good and evil" (Genesis 3:5).[5]

> Have this mind among yourselves, which is yours in Christ Jesus, who, though he was in the form of God, did not count equality with God a thing to be grasped, but emptied himself, taking the form of a servant, being born in the likeness of men. And being found in human form he humbled himself and became obedient unto death, even death on a cross.
>
> PHILIPPIANS 2:5-8

As Joseph Cardinal Ratzinger has put it, "Man can become God, not by making himself God [as he attempted to do in Genesis 3], but by allowing himself to be made 'Son'." It was in the gesture of the Son's obedience that the kingdom or rule of God was realized.[6]

Human creatures dared to disobey the express command of their Creator, and they found themselves utterly unable to bring about reconciliation with him. As an act of merciful justice, the Son of God became man so that as both God and man he could reconcile the two and restore the filial relationship that God originally had offered Adam and Eve. Because of the Incarnation, man's dignity as sons and daughters of God was restored. Because of the Incarnation, God himself entered into his material creation and now relates to it in an entirely new and more intimate way. All this will have great significance for Christian efforts to picture the end times and the concomitant new creation. Because of the Incarnation, the earthly, the concrete, the human, and the symbolic all become especially fitting source material for the images and visions of Revelation.

How does God's incarnate Son go about reconciling God and man in a concrete way? From differing perspectives the four Gospels provide distinct accounts of Jesus' ministry, death, and resurrection, by which humans are saved from their hopeless alienation from God. However, their basic portrait of who Jesus is and how he saved us is mutually consistent and complementary to a surprising degree. All the Gospels portray Jesus as acting as Son of God and as God's anointed (Messiah or Christ); as preaching the Good News about the imminence of God's salvation and kingdom; as forgiving sins, preaching repentance, healing the sick, having authority over Satan and his spirits, and so on. All the Gospels find their climax in Jesus' self-offering and bloody sacrifice on the cross—"for our sins" and "according to the scriptures"—and in his resurrection from the dead, by which he overcame death (see 1 Corinthians 15:3-4). All the Gospels demonstrate how, through Jesus, God overcame the result of sin, man's alienation from God.

Our Part

Contrary to some simplistic promises of "cheap grace," however, one's salvation by Jesus cannot simply be passively presumed, even after a profound initial act of faith in Jesus as one's Savior. The New Testament as a whole, and not only the Gospels, insists that the human choice and obedience that was at the heart of the Old Testament message of salvation is still required. The challenge of Deuteronomy remains: "See, I have set before you this day life and good, death and evil" (Deuteronomy 30:15). If God's people obey God and follow his ways, they shall find life and blessing.

> But if your heart turns away, and you will not hear, …you shall perish…I call heaven and earth to witness against you this day, that I have set before you life and death, blessing and curse; therefore choose life, that you and your descendants may live, loving the LORD your God, obeying his voice, and cleaving to him.
>
> DEUTERONOMY 30:17, 18, 19-20

In the same way, Paul argues in the Letter to the Romans:

> For [God] will render to every man according to his works: to those who by patience in well-doing seek for glory and honor and immortality, he will give eternal life; but for those who are factious and do not obey the truth, but obey wickedness, there will be wrath and fury.
>
> ROMANS 2:6-8

From "the beginning" in human creation to the "new creation" in Jesus, even until the present, the drama of human freedom in response to God's offer of love and adoption as his sons and daughters is ongoing. Will humans accept

God's offer, now made in Jesus, to be his adopted sons and daughters in a loving but obedient relationship to "our Father"? Or will humans continue to try to "be like God, knowing good and evil"?

God respects our dignity and freedom and our decisions and choices. In the Old Testament, obedience to God brought life and blessing; disobedience brought death and curse. What this means in the long run becomes clearer with the fuller revelation in Jesus in the New Testament. If we say yes to God and his commandments, we shall share in God's happiness forever in heaven. If we say no to God and choose our own will over God's, he will respect our decision and leave us to our own autonomous existence separate from him forever.

This, of course, is the essence of existence in hell. As C. S. Lewis put it, "There are only two kinds of people in the end: those who say to God, 'Thy will be done,' and those to whom God says, 'Thy will be done.'"[7] Apart from this drama of the meaning and consequences of human free choices and decisions, the Book of Revelation and other apocalyptic writings make little sense.

End Times in the "Little Apocalypses" in the Gospels

A prominent part of Jesus' teaching during his earthly ministry proclaimed the end and goal of existence in this world. Each of the Synoptic Gospels—Mark, Matthew, and Luke—features a special set of sayings (in the form of a sermon) by Jesus about what believers can expect at the end of the present age. A good place to begin our study of his message about the end times is with the apocalyptic speeches and prophecies of Jesus reported in Matthew 24–25, Luke 17 and especially 21, and Mark 13.

The versions of Jesus' teaching about the end times in Matthew 24 and Luke 21 both follow the basic outline of Mark 13. Matthew's account follows Mark's closely but also is the only one to add a set of parables about the end and the very important story of the Last or general Judgment, and Luke 21 provides chronological "adjustments" to the scenario of Mark 13 (and Matthew 24). So we shall focus first on Matthew 24–25 to present the most complete general end times scenario, and then on Luke 21 for the way in which it distinguishes discreet periods in the end times leading up to the Last Day. Whereas Mark and Matthew seem to imply a close link between the traumatic fall of Jerusalem (A.D. 70) and the final coming of the Son of Man in power, or possibly even an identification of those two events, Luke 21 clearly inserts between them at least one intermediate period, the "times of the Gentiles" (see Luke 21:24).

A scene in which Jesus' followers admire the temple introduces all three accounts of the last days. In response to their admiration of the temple, Jesus prophesies that not one stone will be left upon another, but all will be thrown down (see Matthew 24:2; Mark 13:2; Luke 21:6). The disciples then ask two questions that lead into Jesus' "apocalyptic discourse." Their first question is "Tell us, when will this be?" (Matthew 24:3). This question *when* refers initially to the destruction of the temple just predicted.

The second question in all three accounts asks what warning sign there will be, a question that is related in differing ways to the question about when the temple will be destroyed. In Mark and Luke, both questions apparently relate to the temple's destruction: "Tell us, when will this be, and what will be the sign when these things are all to be accomplished?" (Mark 13:4; see Luke 21:7).

In Matthew, however, the second question explicitly goes beyond the fall of the temple to the coming or parousia of Jesus and to the ending of the age: "Tell us, when will this be, and what will be the sign of your coming and of the close of the age?" (Matthew 24:3b, emphasis added). That the disciples asked the question in this way gives the impression that the fall of Jerusalem and the glorious second coming of Jesus and the end of the age are basically one complex scenario of expected related happenings. Jesus' answer to these questions when and by what sign begins the actual lengthy sermon about the end times in all three Gospels.

Curiosity About the End Times

It must be human nature to be curious about when the end times will come and what are the signs by which we can forecast their coming. Contemporary end time scenarios are not only the featured component of many contemporary Bible studies, sermons, and even best-selling novels. Even at the time of Jesus and the beginnings of the Church, there were widespread rumors about the end times and messianic pretenders. Shortly after the Jewish War, which resulted in the destruction of the temple and of Jerusalem in A.D. 70, a Jewish writer, Josephus, who had observed the final siege of Jerusalem, described the numerous messianic pretenders and prophets who had stirred up the Jewish people to rebel against the rule of the Roman Empire. Perhaps in view of the disastrous result of following false prophets, Jesus' first reported response to the disciples' questions about when the end times would come and by what signs they would be foreshadowed is his emphatic caution against being led astray by false messiahs and false signs.

Thus in Matthew 24, Jesus begins his response to the disciples by refusing to answer their questions directly. Instead he warns them not to be misled by the many pretenders who will come in his name or claim to be the messiah. Those pretenders will lead many astray. Nor should the disciples be alarmed by wars and rumors of wars, "for this must take place, but the end is not yet" (Matthew 24:6). First will come wars among nations, famines and earthquakes, but they are only the beginning of the "birth-pangs" (24:7-8).

Apocalyptic scenarios commonly use the image of "birth pangs." That term implies that the end is in fact a new beginning, the birth of a new order, but that it is ushered in by the most common intense form of suffering known at that time, a woman's labor pains. Nevertheless, these signs are of little or no help in calculating precisely when the end times might come, because every age has wars, famines, and earthquakes.

The Promise of Persecution

Next Jesus gives a very important prophecy—one that the Left Behind series and rapture theories seem to be trying to avoid (at least subconsciously). He makes a categorical prediction that is virtually a promise: that "you" (Jesus' followers) will endure intense persecution (see Matthew 24:9 calls it tribulation) and hatred among the nations because of Jesus' name. At this part of the sermon, only Matthew includes that as a result of this persecution many Christians will fall away and betray and hate one another (see Matthew 24:10). False prophets will make this disunity and strife among Christians even worse (see 24:11), and "because wickedness is multiplied, most men's love will grow cold" (24:12). Jesus' followers will not be spared "the tribulation" and persecution, as rapture theories promise. They will not even be spared widespread falsehood and apostasy from fellow Christians. Jesus' promise in the face of this coming suffering is only that the one "who endures to the end will be saved" (24:13).

A very important prophecy in Matthew 24 is that first the good news about God's kingdom will be preached to all nations throughout the world, "and then the end will come" (Matthew 24:14b). This inserts a significant delay between the fall of Jerusalem and the end. Yet already in the early fifth century St. Jerome was confident that the gospel had spread sufficiently for the end to take place.

After this aside Matthew 24:15 returns to the topic of the sufferings accompanying the destruction of the temple. Jesus repeats a mysterious phrase found also in Mark 13:14, "the abomination of desolation" (my literal translation), but adds an explanation. Mark 13:14 reads, "But *when you see the abomination of desolation standing where it ought not—let the reader understand*—then those in Judea should flee to the mountains" (my translation, emphasis added). In Mark this is clearly meant to be a mysterious saying, an expression in code about the identity of the abomination and about where it is placed, with a reminder to the reader about the need to decipher the code. Such code language is not uncommon in apocalyptic writings. Compare the mysterious number 666 in Revelation and its similar call for readers to decipher the code: "This calls for wisdom: let him who has understanding reckon the number of the beast, for it is a human number, its number is six hundred and sixty-six" (Revelation 13:18).

Matthew apparently does not assume, to the extent that Mark does, that his readers know the answers to the code. He specifies that the Old Testament origin of this mysterious phrase, *abomination of desolation*, is in Daniel. Matthew 24:15 thus interprets that phrase: "When therefore you see the abomination of desolation that *was mentioned by Daniel the prophet standing in the holy place*—let the reader understand" (my translation, emphasis added).

The reference is to Daniel 9:27, 11:31, and 12:11. Daniel 9:27 refers to the desecration of the temple by the Greek Emperor in 167 B.C.:

> And he shall make a strong covenant with many for one week; and for half of the week he shall cause sacrifice and offering to cease; and upon the wing of abominations shall come one who makes desolate, until the decreed end is poured out on the desolator.

Even clearer anticipations of the actual phrase *abomination of desolation* are found in Daniel 11:31—"And they shall set up the *abomination* that makes *desolate*"—and Daniel 12:11—"the *abomination* that makes *desolate*."

Immediately after mentioning the "abomination of desolation," Matthew 24:16-18 (and parallels) reports Jesus' urgent directive for those in Judea to flee to the mountains, for those on rooftops not to try to take anything from the house, and for those in the field not to turn back for their cloaks. Ezekiel 7:16 likewise mentioned escaping to mountains from siege-induced famine and the sword: "And if any survivors escape, they will be on the mountains, like doves of the valleys, all of them moaning, every one over his iniquity." Many patristic writers later considered the Christians' flight to the mountainous area of Pella before the siege of Jerusalem as a fulfillment of this prophecy.[8]

Cosmic Catastrophe

All three Gospel sermons continue to stress urgent and dire conditions. They repeat Jesus' "woe" to those who are with child or who give suck in those days, and Matthew's version recommends prayer that these things not take place in the winter nor on the sabbath (implying a Jewish concern about not being able to flee the disasters without violating the sabbath):

> For then there will be great tribulation, such as has not been from the beginning of the world until now, no, and never will be. And if those days had not been shortened, no human being would be saved; but for the sake of the elect those days will be shortened.
>
> MATTHEW 24:21-22

These horrors all seem associated in Matthew's version with the "abomination of desolation" in the temple, probably already a horrific past event by the time Matthew wrote down his Gospel.

Also evidently relating to the sufferings accompanying Jerusalem's destruction comes a repetition of warnings against false messiahs and about false prophets who perform even "signs and wonders" so as to lead the chosen people astray. Revelation 13 will similarly describe the second beast as a false prophet who can work lying wonders. This theme goes back to Deuteronomy 13:1-3, which warns that even some prophets who work wonders might nevertheless be preaching an idolatrous message.

Jesus firmly warns his followers not to believe claims that the messiah is in some particular location, nor to go hastening to that spot in attempts to find him. For the parousia or coming of the Son of Man will take place like a flash of lightning across the entire sky. It will be visible to everyone and cannot be missed or mistaken. He adds the maxim "Wherever the body is, there the eagles will be gathered together" (Matthew 24:28). After a disaster takes place, its location will be obvious: One can find it by going to the place where the vultures are gathering. Jesus discourages speculation not only about when these prophecies will be fulfilled but also about where.

Because it is hard to imagine what cosmic catastrophes in the distant future will look like, later biblical texts tend to reuse earlier biblical images to describe them, as if these images were "apocalyptic stage props."[9] Thus Matthew 24 and Mark 13 (and, as we shall see, Revelation) rely heavily on images in the Old Testament prophets to portray the Day of the Lord on which he will judge the sins of humans. To differing extents, both Matthew's and Mark's sermons relate the cosmic signs associated with the return of Jesus to the aftermath of the tribulation in Jerusalem.

Matthew's account seems to link them closely: "Immediately after the tribulation of those days the sun will be darkened, and the moon will not give its light, and the stars will fall from heaven, and the powers of the heavens will be shaken" (Matthew 24:29). The sermon recalls the words of Old Testament prophets, such as the prophecy about the woes associated with the Day of the Lord in Isaiah 13:9-13:

> For the stars of the heavens and their constellations will not give their light; the sun will be dark at its rising and the moon will not shed its light.... Therefore I will make the heavens tremble, and the earth will be shaken out of its place, at the wrath of the LORD of hosts in the day of his fierce anger.
>
> ISAIAH 13:10, 13

To describe the actual and climactic coming of the Son of Man in glory, Mark 13:26 for the most part simply quotes from Daniel 7:13, "And then they will see the Son of man coming in clouds," but adds the details "with great power and glory" (Mark 13:26). Matthew's version puts even more emphasis on accompanying signs, but otherwise it follows Mark's closely:

> *Then will appear the sign of the Son of man in heaven, and then all the tribes of the earth will mourn* [see Zechariah 12:10], and they will see the Son of man coming on the clouds of heaven with power and great glory; and he will send out his angels *with a loud trumpet call*, and they will gather his elect from the four winds, from one end of heaven to the other.
>
> MATTHEW 24:30-31, emphasis added

Preparation Parables

One would expect the narrative of the Last Judgment to follow immediately after this gathering of the elect, but in both Matthew and Mark, the sermon first inserts a parable of the fig tree and a second teaching concerning the timing of the *parousia* (see Matthew 24:32-36; Mark 13:28-32). In addition, Matthew adds parables about keeping watch lest a thief enter one's house (see Matthew 24:42-44), about the behavior of servants during their master's absence (see 24:45-51), about the five wise and five foolish virgins (see 25:1-13), plus the parable of the talents (see 25:14-30). Only then does Matthew narrate Jesus' prophecy about the Last Judgment (see 25:31-46), which concludes the sermon about the end times.

Thus Matthew's sermon pauses, as it were, after describing the signs of the Son of Man and his publicly observable return on the clouds. Matthew's sermon prepares his readers for the Last Judgment with some parables about signs and the suddenness of the Son of Man's coming. The first of these parables is that when the fig tree puts forth leaves, people know that summer is near. Similarly, when people see these things, they should know that the Son of Man is very near. "Truly, I say to you, this generation will not pass away till all these things take place" (Matthew 24:34). In fact, the generation alive in Jesus' day did see the prophesied destruction of Jerusalem but not the fulfillment of prophecies about Jesus' end time appearance. This may explain why Luke's version of this sermon takes great care to distinguish between different periods, one relating to the fall of Jerusalem and another to Jesus' return at the end, as well as to intervening stages between them.

After the statement about this generation's witnessing these events, both Matthew's and Mark's versions immediately add the caution, "But of that day and hour no one knows, not even the angels of heaven, nor the Son, but the Father only" (Matthew 24:36). A stronger caution against computing end time scenarios could hardly be found. Jesus claims that in his human nature not even he has been given to know "that day and hour." Shocking as this assertion has been for many who believe in Jesus' divinity, it illustrates the truth of Paul's statement, "He emptied himself, taking the form of a slave" (Philippians 2:7, my translation). Compare Luke 2:52, "And Jesus increased in wisdom and in stature."

Both of these verses help explain human ignorance in Jesus.

The sermons go on to compare the suddenness of the Son of Man's coming with how unexpected was the flood in Noah's time.

> As were the days of Noah, so will be the coming of the Son of man. For as in those days before the flood they were eating and drinking, marrying and giving in marriage, until the day when Noah entered the ark, and they did not know until the flood came and swept them all away, so will be the coming of the Son of man.
>
> MATTHEW 24:37-39

The vast majority of people will be going about their daily occupations when the Son of Man suddenly appears. Even though his coming has been plainly prophesied, it will come unexpectedly upon most people, who will remain unprepared for it.

To describe the unexpectedness of the parousia, Jesus uses a comparison that in the last couple of centuries has fueled theories that true believers will be "raptured" to heaven so that they will be spared the tribulation that precedes his second coming.

> Then two men will be in the field; one is taken and one is left. Two women will be grinding at the mill; one is taken and one is left. Watch therefore, for you do not know on what day your Lord is coming.
>
> MATTHEW 24:40-42

In the context in Matthew, however, the point is clear that imagery about the unpredictable selection among pairs of people does not support a theory about a rapture of believers from among others who are "left behind." Its emphasis is rather on the total unpredictability of the time at which "your Lord is coming" (Matthew 24:42). "Therefore you also must be ready, *for the Son of man is coming at an hour you do not expect*" (24:44, emphasis added). The context for this taking of one person and leaving of another is without doubt the second coming itself of the Son of Man at the end of time.

The following parable about faithful and unfaithful servants in Matthew 24:45-51 sounds a special warning not to presume that "my master is delayed" and therefore abuse one's fellow servants and carouse with drunkards. The master will return "at an hour [the abusive servant] does not know" and will punish him in the place in which "men will weep and gnash their teeth" (24:50-51). "Weeping and gnashing of teeth" is a common symbol for hell, especially in Matthew (see Matthew 8:12; 13:42, 50; 22:13; 24:51; 25:30; Luke 13:28).

The parable of the five wise and five foolish maidens in Matthew 25:1-13 reinforces the need for Christ's followers to be ready at all times for the delayed but sudden return of the absent bridegroom. It ends with a similar conclusion: "Watch therefore, for you know neither the day nor the hour" (Matthew 25:13).

The next parable, that of the talents, illustrates what Jesus' followers are to do during his absence while awaiting his return. All of them are entrusted with sums of money that they are expected to administrate for the master in his absence. The amounts differ according to the abilities of the recipients. Those who use the money to trade for profit are welcomed "into the joy of [their] master" (an obvious symbol for heaven). The servant who out of fear simply hides the money without earning more with it is stripped of that money and cast out as a worthless servant "into the outer darkness; there men will weep and gnash their teeth" (Matthew 25:30).

The parable implies that we are to work with the talents God gives us and to put them to productive use during the time that we have before Jesus' return (and more immediately, before our death, which cuts short every person's time). Even though the situation in which we work is no longer idyllic, as it was in Genesis, the parable recalls God's primeval commission for humans to work the earth and garden in which he placed them (Genesis 1–2).

Our efforts or failure to perform our assigned tasks in this intermediate time of the master's absence will carry enormous consequences: Either we will enter the joy of the master (heaven), or we will be cast into the outer darkness (hell). The instructions of Jesus regarding how we are to prepare for his return (in judgment) focus entirely on our exercising our talents and working productively during our time before this return. Futile efforts to calculate the circumstances of Jesus' return waste precious time, which instead Paul would have us use to "work out [our] own salvation with fear and trembling" (Philippians 2:12).

Prophetic Periods

Neither the Markan nor Matthean version of Jesus' speech about the end times distinguishes very clearly between the traumatic events of the destruction of Jerusalem and the happenings that lead up to the second coming of Jesus and the definitive end of the world. Perhaps Luke is aware of confusion or disillusionment among some Christians, because their anticipation that Jesus would return in judgment and that the world would end was not fulfilled in the period shortly following the destruction of the temple and Jerusalem, as the wording of both Mark 13 and Matthew 24–25 might have led them to expect. The Lukan version of Jesus' speech inserts several intermediate periods between the fall of Jerusalem and the end.

Both Matthew 24:6 and Mark 13:7 instruct the disciples not to be alarmed at "wars and rumors of wars...for this must take place, but the end is not yet." Luke 21:9 is similar: "This must *first* take place, but the end *will not be at once*" (emphasis added). All three versions then foretell that "nation will rise against nation" and that there will be famines and earthquakes. But Luke 21:11 replaces the apocalyptic reference and the conclusion of Mark 13:8 and Matthew 24:8 that "this is but the beginning of the birth-pangs" with the more general "and there will be terrors and great signs from heaven."

Whereas Matthew and Mark can give the impression that it is during this period of wars and heavenly signs that Christians will be persecuted in councils and synagogues (see Matthew 24:9; Mark 13:9), Luke clarifies that this period of persecution will take place *before* all these wars and signs from heaven: "But before all this they will lay their hands on you and persecute you.... This will be a time for you to bear testimony" (Luke 21:12, 13).

In other words, in Luke it is much clearer than in Mark and Matthew that not one but two distinct periods are here being foretold. First comes a period of persecution in synagogues (a period which Luke narrates in the Acts of the Apostles). After this season of persecution comes the time of wars and rumors of wars, and of famines and other disasters, which Mark and Matthew also mention. Historically the Roman-Jewish war and destruction of Jerusalem did take place after the persecutions recorded in the Acts of the Apostles.

Luke also diverges from the emphasis of Mark and Matthew regarding the destruction of Jerusalem and its temple. Luke 21:20 drops the Markan and Matthean apocalyptic code language about the "abomination of desolation set up where it ought not be (let the reader understand)." Luke replaces this code expression with a straightforward prediction: "But when you see Jerusalem surrounded by armies, then know that its desolation has come near." He also treats the fall of Jerusalem as a distinct period of fulfilled prophecy: "For these are days of vengeance, to fulfill all that is written" (Luke 21:22).

The speech in Mark and Matthew pronounces woes on those with child and those breast-feeding in the days of tribulation, which will be worse than any from the beginning to the end of time (see Mark 13:17-19, Matthew 24:19-21). Luke 21:23-24 contextualizes these woes not within end time tribulations, as they seem to be in Mark and Matthew, but as a part of Jerusalem's punishment, which was promised by the prophets. Then will follow another historical period of Jewish exile and of continued pagan domination over Jerusalem in a protracted time of the Gentiles.

> For great distress shall be upon the earth and wrath upon this people; they will fall by the edge of the sword, and be led captive among all nations; and Jerusalem will be trodden down by the Gentiles, until the times of the Gentiles are fulfilled.
>
> LUKE 21:23b-24

Mark 13:24-27 and Matthew 24:29-31 do not specify distinct subunits within the period of tribulation related to the fall of Jerusalem, which would be followed by the coming of false messiahs and cosmic signs and Jesus' return in glory to gather the elect before the final judgment. Luke specifies at least three periods related to these prophecies. After the periods of punishment of Jerusalem and the times of the Gentiles, Luke 21:25-27 mentions the time of cosmic signs and stress, during which the Son of Man will be seen returning in glory on a cloud. At the onset of cosmic signs, Luke 21:28 says, "look up and raise your heads, because your redemption is drawing near." Luke 21:29-33 then reports the parable of the fig tree, as do Mark 13 and Matthew 24, after which Luke concludes the entire speech with Jesus' warning not to let one's heart be weighed down by dissipation and the cares of life but to watch and pray so as to be ready to face the Son of Man (Luke 21:34-36).

Thus within the prophecies of Jerusalem's fall and the end of the world in Mark 13 and Matthew 24, Luke distinguishes at least the following subunits or periods of time: Chronologically first will come a time of *persecution* (Luke 21:12-19), which Luke reports in the Acts of the Apostles. Next, in order, come a time of *false prophets and messiahs* (21:8-9); a period of *wars and earthquakes and famines and terrors from heaven* (21:9-11); the siege and *destruction of Jerusalem* (21:20-24); followed by a period called *"the times of the Gentiles"* (21:24b); and finally the period of *cosmic signs* and the return of Jesus in power and glory (21:25-28). The concluding exhortation in this Lukan version of Jesus' apocalyptic speech is to be alert and not be distracted by the lures and cares of daily life, so the disciples can face Jesus returning as their judge.

More than the apocalyptic speeches in Mark and Matthew, Luke's version clearly distinguishes the tribulations surrounding the fall of Jerusalem from several other periods before and after. Luke presents the following progression: persecution, false prophets, wars and natural disasters, the fall of Jerusalem, the times of the Gentiles, and finally the cosmic signs and Jesus' return or parousia as judge. This protects from disillusionment those who might have expected that the end of time would follow shortly after the fall of Jerusalem. Before the end of time there will be a period of unspecified duration called the "times of the Gentiles," within which readers of Luke and Acts up to the twenty-first century can situate themselves. The only predictions from these apocalyptic expectations that remain to be fulfilled are the cosmic signs and Jesus' final return.

Matthew 25: The Final Judgment

After teaching about what he expects of his followers during the time of his absence before his return, Jesus in Matthew turns to the climactic final public judgment of the entire world that will take place when he returns in glory. This final judgment is God's ultimate answer to the problem of evil in the world and to how humans have exercised the freedom with which God endowed them when he offered them a share in his own divine and Trinitarian life as his adopted sons and daughters. Though humans' initial reconciliation with God requires the blood of the incarnate Lamb of God, their ultimate salvation or damnation depends in addition on how they use their freedom after Jesus has justified them.

In the Last Judgment, Christ the judge will separate individuals from all the nations "one from another as a shepherd separates the sheep from the goats" (Matthew 25:32). To the "sheep" on his right hand Jesus will give the invitation, "Come, O blessed of my Father, inherit the kingdom prepared for you from the foundation of the world" (25:34). To the "goats" on his left he will say: "Depart from me, you cursed, into the eternal fire prepared for the devil and his angels" (25:41).

Some humans will be saved and others damned, depending on how they used their freedom in response to the opportunities God offered them. The biblical drama of human freedom and sin, repentance or hardening of hearts, and corresponding reward or punishment begins in Genesis 3. It persists through the turbulent history of God's people until the sending of his Son, then to the people's free response to God's Son and to his disciples and to his body the Church. This biblical drama continues until the end of days and the final judgment.

The consequences of this drama of human freedom are almost unimaginable in their categorical gravity: "And they will go away into eternal punishment, but the righteous into eternal life" (Matthew 25:46). Choices that humans make in response to God and to his commands and invitations have eternal consequences, for complete happiness or for damnation.

In the portrayal of the Last Judgment in Matthew 25, the criterion for judgment is how each person treats other humans. "Truly, I say to you, *as you did it to one of the least of these my brethren, you did it to me*" (Matthew 25:40, emphasis added; see 25:45). For Jesus identifies "the least of these my brethren" with himself, as he also does when he appears to Paul: "Saul, Saul, why do you persecute me?" (Acts 9:4). St. Paul explains this identification by his analogy of the body of Christ, of which we Christians are members: "Now you are the body of Christ and individually members of it" (1 Corinthians 12:27; compare 1 Corinthians 12:12-13; Ephesians 4:15-16; Romans 12:4-8; and John 15, where Christ is the vine and his disciples are the branches).

The chasm between God the Creator and the human creatures who dared to challenge and disobey him was bridged through God's pure grace and mercy by the Word's becoming flesh (see John 1:14). As Adam represented all his human descendants in his disobedience and brought death to all men, the Second Adam won resurrection and eternal life for us (see Romans 5:17-19) through his obedience "unto death, even death on a cross" (Philippians 2:8). In baptism, Christians die with Christ to sin and rise with Christ to eternal life (see Romans 6:3-11; Colossians 2:12-13). Through baptism, Christians receive the Holy Spirit and become incorporated into Christ's body, the Church. Ultimately, this incorporation into Christ helps explain why Jesus can say at the Last Judgment, "Truly, I say to you, as you did it to one of the least of these my brethren, you did it to me" (Matthew 25:40).

The stakes cannot be higher. The gravity of Jesus' message about the Last Judgment is definitive. It recalls the life-and-death, yes-or-no challenge of Deuteronomy: "I call heaven and earth to witness against you this day, that I have set before you life and death, blessing and curse; therefore choose life, that you and your descendants may live"

(Deuteronomy 30:19). But at the Last Judgment the consequences of human choices are not merely earthly life or death, nor life either in the Promised Land or in exile, but eternal life in heaven or the spiritual death of eternal separation from God, for whom every fiber of our being longs.

Recalling Augustine's words again, "You have made us for yourself, O God, and our hearts are restless until they rest in you."[10] If we do not rest eternally in God in heaven, we will be eternally frustrated and tormented by the lack of that good for which we were created. This is the sobering reality of which Jesus reminds us in his account of the Last Judgment, which brings the final days to their culmination.

Conclusion

All three Gospel accounts of Jesus' speech about the end times and Jesus' return emphasize the tribulation and need for faithful endurance that Christians must expect, especially because of hostility from those who rebel against God. The horrific destruction of Jerusalem and its temple symbolize the sufferings from wars and famines and natural disorders, as well as persecution, that Christians will face at the end of time as prelude to God's inauguration of his kingdom. All three accounts use apocalyptic language and the symbolism of cosmic signs and catastrophes to emphasize the intensity of suffering associated with the new creation and the coming of the kingdom of God (which Mark and Matthew call "birth-pangs"). All three emphasize our need to be ready for the final tribulation and judgment. We must not let preoccupation with daily cares and concerns leave us unprepared.

What the Lukan version adds to the general apocalyptic expectations in Mark and Matthew is the "periodization" or separation of these expectations for the final days into distinct and consecutive periods. Although the destruction of the temple and Jerusalem can provide a powerful symbol of the sufferings of the end times, Luke establishes that they are distinct from the final tribulations. Between the fall of Jerusalem in A.D. 70 and the cosmic signs that portend the ultimate end of historical time will come periods of Jewish exile, foreign domination of Jerusalem, and "times of the Gentiles."

These distinctions help answer questions arising from Christian perplexity over the identification of the catastrophes of Jerusalem with those at the end of the world. From the horrors of the punishment of Jerusalem, Christians can learn the severity of the coming tribulations at the end of time. However, the horrors of the end time tribulations need not undermine Christian hope in God, no matter how terrible their circumstances. "Now when these things begin to take place, look up and raise your heads, because your redemption is drawing near" (Luke 21:28).

Notes:

1. Elder Mullan, trans., "Second Week, Contemplation on the Incarnation," from *Spiritual Exercises of St. Ignatius of Loyola*, URL http://www.ccel.org/i/ignatius/exercises/exercises.html, accessed July 17, 2003.

2. My translation of the Hebrew in light of the Greek and Latin translations.

3. My translation; see Genesis 26:4.

4. St. Athanasius, *On the Incarnation,* a religious of C.S.M.V., trans. (Crestwood, N.Y.: St. Vladimir's, 1993), 93.

5. Paul regularly ignores Eve when he contrasts the first and second Adam.

6. Joseph Ratzinger, *Eschatology: Death and Eternal Life*, Michael Waldstein, trans. (Washington, D.C.: Catholic University of America Press, 1988), 64-65.

7. C. S. Lewis, *The Great Divorce* (New York: Macmillan, 1946), 72.

8. See St. Thomas Aquinas, *Catena aurea in quatuor evangelia* (Rome: Marietti, 1953), 348-49.

9. See John Randall, *The Book of Revelation: What Does It Really Say?* (Locust Valley, N.Y.: Living Flame Press, 1976), 33-36.

10. Augustine, *Confessions*, 1.1.

chapter four

The End Times in the Pauline Letters

As we have noted throughout the previous chapters, Paul's letters contain many references to Jesus' final return. His exaltation of Jesus as "the new Adam" and his assurances about resurrection from the dead provide valuable insight for some preliminary answers to our question "What does the Bible say about the end times?"

Adam's Sin Reversed: Philippians 2
The reasons God must keep giving humans so many harsh and dramatic warnings go back ultimately to the original ambition of Adam and Eve to be as God. The rebellion that Adam began continued with his descendants and spread throughout the world in all areas of life. Thus God and his prophets had constantly to correct and even to threaten his wayward children in order to bring them back to his ways. As Paul so compellingly argues, it took the obedience of the New Adam, the Son of God himself become man, to undo decisively the damage of Adam's sin of disobedience:

> Have this mind among yourselves, which is yours in Christ Jesus, who, though he was in the form of God, did not count equality with God a thing to be grasped, but emptied himself, taking the form of a servant, being born in the likeness of men. And being found in human form he humbled himself and became obedient unto death, even death on a cross.
>
> PHILIPPIANS 2:5-8

Recently scholars have debated whether this passage refers to the human Jesus' reversing Adam's disobedience by his obedience or to the preexistent Son of God's emptying himself in the Incarnation. Throughout the centuries many Catholic interpreters have recognized both patterns in it. Both the preexistent and the incarnate Son refrained from grasping at equal status with God. The preexistent Son emptied himself initially in the Incarnation; the incarnate second Adam further emptied himself by becoming obedient even unto death, reversing Adam's ambitious disobedience.

This two-edged pattern pertains at least to settings in which Philippians 2 is read in light of other New Testament passages, especially other Pauline passages. For example, 2 Corinthians 8:9 tells us, "Though [Jesus] was rich, yet for your sake he became poor, so that by his poverty you might become rich." Given the fact that Jesus was merely a carpenter in Nazareth, it seems implausible to understand his "having been rich" in any other manner than as a reference to his preexistence as divine. Compare also Colossians 1:15, 19-20:

> He is the image of the invisible God, the first-born of all
> creation.... For in him all the fulness of God was pleased
> to dwell, and through him to reconcile to himself all
> things, whether on earth or in heaven, making peace by
> the blood of his cross.

Other New Testament passages that imply preexistence followed by voluntary incarnation and suffering enrich the theological context for interpreting this passage in Philippians. Among these is the prologue of John's Gospel: "In the beginning was the Word, and the Word was with God, and the Word was God. He was in the beginning with God.... And the Word became flesh and dwelt among us" (John 1:1-2, 14). Compare John 17:5: "And now, Father, glorify thou me in thy own presence with the glory which I had with thee before the world was made." See also Hebrews 1:3, "He reflects the glory of God and bears the very stamp of his nature, upholding the universe by his word of power. When he had made purification for sins, he sat down at the right hand of the Majesty on high."

Jesus was "in the form of God" (Philippians 2:6) not only in his preexistence as Son within the Trinity but as a human descendant of Adam, who is an "image of God." Even though "in the beginning" God had placed Adam in dominion over the material world, Adam tried to get even more power by grasping at equality with God himself, being able "to know good and evil." In practice, especially since (ironically) evil did not yet exist on earth, knowing good and evil was equivalent to being able to determine for oneself what was right and what was wrong. It meant not being told what to do by someone else, not even by one's Creator.

On both the divine and human levels, Jesus acted in a way that directly countered Adam's attempt to be or to function as God: "He did not count equality with God a thing to be grasped." He voluntarily accepted the form of a slave, obeying God's will. If Philippians implies preexistence (as I believe it does), then the statement that Jesus "emptied himself, taking the form of a slave, being born in the likeness of men" would refer primarily to the incarnation of the Second Person of the Trinity as man. However, it also refers to Jesus' further humiliation as man through obedience "unto death, even death on a cross." Jesus embraced crucifixion, which was reserved for slaves, rebels, and criminals who were not Roman citizens.

God responds to Jesus' self-emptying for our sakes by exalting him as Lord of all creation, thus illustrating one of Jesus' own best-known sayings: "Whoever exalts himself [as Adam tried to do] will be humbled, and whoever humbles himself [as Jesus himself did] will be exalted" (Matthew

23:12). Jesus' self-emptying and God's exaltation of him become the turning point of human history through which the human race is again reconciled to God.

> Therefore God has highly exalted him and bestowed on him the name which is above every name, that at the name of Jesus every knee should bow, in heaven and on earth and under the earth, and every tongue confess that Jesus Christ is Lord, to the glory of God the Father.
>
> PHILIPPIANS 2:9-11

This turning point in history halted the inevitable downward slide of the human race toward hell and prepared for the final triumph of justice at the end of history, when Jesus will return to judge the world. As a result of his self-sacrifice for the sake of all humans, Jesus has amply merited the authority by which he will judge all humans in the end times. Thus in Revelation the heavenly court sings to him, the Lamb who was slain:

> Worthy art thou to take the scroll and to open its seals, for thou wast slain and by thy blood didst ransom men for God from every tribe and tongue and people and nation, and hast made them a kingdom and priests to our God, and they shall reign on earth.
>
> REVELATIONS 5:9-10

The First and Second Adam in Romans

Romans 5–8 further develops Paul's contrast between the first Adam, who brought death to all, and the second Adam, who made possible resurrection for all in a new creation. Paul first emphasizes that

> God shows his love for us in that while we were yet sinners Christ died for us. Since, therefore, we are now justified by his blood, much more shall we be saved by him from the wrath of God. For if while we were enemies we were

> reconciled to God by the death of his Son, much more, now
> that we are reconciled, shall we be saved by his life.
>
> ROMANS 5:8-10

Paul's reference to the "wrath of God" recalls God's many attempts through the prophets to summon his people back to his ways, including his frequent threats that if the people persisted in their sins they would suffer severe punishments. The reference also recalls what Paul emphasized earlier in Romans: that God will judge all humans according to their works and so apportion to them eternal life in either glory or distress.

> But by your hard and impenitent heart you are storing up wrath for yourself on the day of wrath when God's righteous judgment will be revealed. For he will render to every man according to his works: to those who by patience in well-doing seek for glory and honor and immortality, he will give eternal life; but for those who are factious and do not obey the truth, but obey wickedness, there will be wrath and fury. There will be tribulation and distress for every human being who does evil, the Jew first and also the Greek, but glory and honor and peace for every one who does good, the Jew first and also the Greek. For God shows no partiality.
>
> ROMANS 2:5-11

Paul's discussion of how the Law affects the interrelationships of Jews and Gentiles in God's plan of salvation (Romans 2:12–4:25) is less relevant to our purposes than is his clarifying how Christ's saving role as second Adam relates to his return "to judge the living and the dead" (The Apostles' Creed). The revelation that pertains most directly to the end times is that sin and death came into the world through Adam and spread to all men because all men sinned (see Romans 5:12-14). Because sin has to be ultimately judged and death finally overcome, Adam's sin sets the stage for Jesus' return in the end times. Paul explicitly labels Adam as an Old Testament type to which Christ corresponds:

> If, because of one man's trespass, death reigned through that one man, much more will those who receive the abundance of grace and the free gift of righteousness reign in life through the one man Jesus Christ. Then as one man's trespass led to condemnation for all men, so one man's act of righteousness leads to acquittal and life for all men. For as by one man's disobedience many were made sinners, so by one man's obedience many will be made righteous.
>
> ROMANS 5:17-19

The saving role of Jesus as second Adam or as Adam of the end times, who reverses in a new creation the damage done by the original Adam, could not be more emphatically expressed.

The Law in Romans 7

Paul's view of the role of the Law in God's saving plan changed radically after he met the resurrected Christ. He recognized a parallel between God's original commandment to Adam and God's deliverance of his Law to Moses after the Fall. The commandment to Adam and the Law of Moses both came from God himself and both expressed the truth about what is right and what is wrong. Both were therefore good and meant for good:

> What then shall we say? That the law is sin? By no means! Yet, if it had not been for the law, I should not have known sin. I should not have known what it is to covet if the law had not said, "You shall not covet." But sin, finding opportunity in the commandment, wrought in me all kinds of covetousness.
>
> ROMANS 7:7-8a

Both the command to Adam and the Law were meant to save humans from committing actions that would cause them grave harm. However, because of their perverse sense of freedom, both Adam and the chosen people found the commandments of God a challenge to their independence. They did not want their freedom limited, not even by commands from their Creator. As a result, the commands that God gave humans to guide them along the path of life were regarded as offensive limitations and challenges to human desire for freedom and even autonomy. Humans wanted autonomy even from God, as if they too were God.

> Apart from the law sin lies dead. I was once alive apart from the law, but when the commandment came, sin revived and I died; the very commandment which promised life proved to be death to me. For sin, finding opportunity in the commandment, deceived me and by it killed me. So the law is holy, and the commandment is holy and just and good.
>
> ROMANS 7:8b-12

Paul implies that before God gave the command not to eat of the Tree of Knowledge of Good and Evil, Adam was naively innocent of actual disobedience and sin. Before that command Adam had not conceived what it might mean to covet something that he was not supposed to have. In Genesis 3 the serpent used God's commandment as an opportunity to arouse covetousness in man.

After Adam's fall the indwelling tendency to sin stirred up in his descendants an analogous dynamic of resentful autonomy, when they too experienced what they considered limitations by God's law on their freedom, "self-expression," and "choice." In the beginning Adam possessed life without death before and apart from God's command, but he chose sin and therefore was doomed to die. Later, the commandments of the Law aroused a rebellious spirit in God's people, who similarly chose actions leading to death.

The very commandment that promised unending life to Adam if he obeyed proved eventually to lead to Adam's death, because the serpent took the opportunity of its prohibition to deceive him and to bring about death for him and all humans. Similarly, the Law later set forth a choice: "I have set before you life and death, blessing and curse; therefore choose life, that you and your descendants may live" (Deuteronomy 30:19). As the serpent found opportunity in Adam's irritation at the restrictions of God's commandments to deceive him, with fatal consequences, the indwelling tendency to sin after Adam's fall aroused a similar restlessness in Adam's descendants and lured them into committing actions that also resulted in death. In both cases human disobedience changed God's holy and just command into an occasion of death.

Indwelling Sin and Indwelling Spirit: Romans 7–8

> We know that the law is spiritual; but I am carnal, sold under sin. I do not understand my own actions. For I do not do what I want, but I do the very thing I hate. Now if I do what I do not want, I agree that the law is good. So then it is no longer I that do it, but sin which dwells within me.
>
> ROMANS 7:14-17

Paul points out that after Adam's fall his descendents face a greater struggle with temptation than Adam faced in his original innocence. Even though the law is spiritual and good and meant to bring men blessings, Adam's descendants are no longer spiritual but are dominated by the flesh and by sin and therefore unable to keep the law, despite their esteem for it. Paul's reference in Romans 7 to sin dwelling within him parallels his reference in Romans 8 to the Holy Spirit's welling within him (and expelling or overcoming the power of indwelling sin).

This parallel between indwelling sin, which overpowers what Paul desires to do, and the indwelling Spirit, who finally enables him to obey the law's requirements implies that sin functions (and is overcome) as if it were a demon possessing a person. In the Gospels Jesus and his disciples, under the power of the indwelling Holy Spirit, drive out unclean spirits from individuals (see Mark 1:27; 6:7). Similarly in Romans the indwelling Holy Spirit overcomes the power of indwelling sin:

> But you are not in the flesh, you are in the Spirit, if in fact the Spirit of God dwells in you. Any one who does not have the Spirit of Christ does not belong to him. But if Christ is in you, although your bodies are dead because of sin, your spirits are alive because of righteousness.
>
> ROMANS 8:9

From Adam we inherit our status of being wounded by sin and living "according to the flesh." From Christ we receive the indwelling Holy Spirit, so that we are empowered to live "according to the spirit." This Spirit not only overpowers and expels indwelling sin, but it gives our souls life and makes it possible for our bodies to be resurrected at the end times. "If the Spirit of him who raised Jesus from the dead dwells in you, he who raised Christ Jesus from the dead will give life to your mortal bodies also through his Spirit who dwells in you" (Romans 8:11).

> For all who are led by the Spirit of God are sons of God. For you did not receive the spirit of slavery to fall back into fear, but you have received the spirit of sonship. When we cry, "Abba! Father!" it is the Spirit himself bearing witness with our spirit that we are children of God, and if children, then heirs, heirs of God and fellow heirs with Christ, provided we suffer with him in order that we may also be glorified with him.
>
> ROMANS 8:14-17

Christian Hope

The Christian anticipation of being raised with Jesus at the end times does not preclude the need for Christians to live now as sons and daughters of God, in an intimacy with him that enables us to use the term of endearment Abba. Living with the Spirit as God's children frees Christians from fear and fills them with hope that they will share in Jesus' sonship for all eternity (in heaven). However, part of living as sons and daughters of the Father and as brothers and sisters of Jesus is the provision that "we suffer with him in order that we may also be glorified with him" (Romans 8:17b). This Pauline hope does not remotely sound like an expectation that Christians will be "raptured" to heaven so they can escape the suffering of the "great tribulation."

It is precisely because of Christ and his indwelling Holy Spirit that Paul looks forward in hope and without fear to the end times. The sufferings of the present are nothing compared to the glory to be revealed at the end. All creation eagerly awaits the revealing of the sons and daughters of God (see Romans 8:18-19).

> We know that the whole creation has been groaning in travail together until now; and not only the creation, but we ourselves, who have the first fruits of the Spirit, groan inwardly as we wait for adoption as sons, the redemption of our bodies.
>
> ROMANS 8:22-23

Paul's use of birthing language here conveys both pain and hope. Even Christians, in whom the Holy Spirit is dwelling, have not the fullness (that is, not the complete harvest) of the Holy Spirit but only his "first fruits." Therefore, in the present age Christians share in creation's groaning at the birth of the new age and new creation, which will take the form of resurrection of their bodies in the end times. "For in this hope we were saved" (Romans 8:24a).

Paul ends his treatment of the indwelling Holy Spirit with a hymn of praise and unfailing hope:

> Who shall separate us from the love of Christ? Shall tribulation, or distress, or persecution, or famine, or nakedness, or peril, or sword? As it is written, 'For thy sake we are being killed all the day long; we are regarded as sheep to be slaughtered.' No, in all these things we are more than conquerors through him who loved us. For I am sure that neither death, nor life, nor angels, nor principalities, nor things present, nor things to come, nor powers, nor height, nor depth, nor anything else in all creation, will be able to separate us from the love of God in Christ Jesus our Lord.
>
> ROMANS 8:35-39

Far from anticipating that Christians will avoid horrible suffering as the end times draw near, Paul fully expects that Christians will undergo "tribulation, or distress, or persecution, or famine, or nakedness, or peril, or sword." He applies to Christians the message of Psalm 44:22: "For thy sake we are slain all the day long, and accounted as sheep for the slaughter." Paul sees his own suffering and that of other Christians as badges of honor, not something we hope to be spared by being raptured to heaven before the tribulation begins.

Paul gives clear direction on how to approach the end times. We are to hope to share in Christ's glory and victory, after willingly and courageously sharing his rejection by the world and his suffering. We are not to live in fear of the expected tribulation. We are to trust that nothing we face will be able to "separate us from the love of Christ."

The Two Adams and Bodily Resurrection in 1 Corinthians 15

A pivotal part of Paul's hope for the end times is grounded in the resurrection of our bodies as a result of the action of the risen Christ, whom he portrays as the second Adam.

Paul clarifies this hope especially in 1 Corinthians 15. There he is writing to a Greek community whose cultural sensitivities make them open to believing that human souls are immortal and live on after death, more than that human bodies can be resurrected and be reunited with these immortal souls. Paul demonstrates the Corinthians' inconsistency in denying that bodily resurrection is possible, for their very conversion to Christianity depends on their belief in the Good News that Jesus was indeed resurrected from the dead.

To demonstrate this, Paul must reaffirm and explain the meaning and implications of the very early creed that converts, including himself, accepted when they became Christians. Christ's resurrection provides Christians hope that we, like Christ, will be raised from the dead. To explain this, Paul once more contrasts how all humans die because of Adam's sin with how all can hope to be resurrected in Christ, who is the Adam of the new creation. This explanation lays the groundwork for Paul's portrayal of the absolute end of time, when all things, even death, will be put under Christ's feet. When all things are finally subjected to Christ, "then the Son himself will also be subjected to him who put all things under him, that God may be everything to everyone" (or "all in all") (1 Corinthians 15:28).

The Grounding of Christian Faith in Christ's Resurrection

Paul begins his teaching on bodily resurrection by reminding his community of the gospel that he preached to them, because of which they became Christians and on which their salvation rests:

> For I *delivered* to you as of first importance what I also *received*, that Christ died for our sins in accordance with the scriptures, that he was buried, that he was raised on

> the third day in accordance with the scriptures, and that
> he appeared to Cephas, then to the twelve.
>
> 1 CORINTHIANS 15:3-5, emphasis added

Paul's terms for "delivering" or "passing on" what he himself received are technical terminology for tradition in both Judaism and Christianity. The instruction that Paul gave to his newly converted Corinthians was not a teaching original to him. Paul taught them the same tradition in which he himself had been instructed after receiving his vision of the risen Christ. Since Paul's experience of the risen Christ took place only two to three years at most after Jesus' death and resurrection, the instruction that he received when he joined the Christian community at Damascus is most probably the very earliest creed of the Church. When the Christians at Damascus (Acts 9:10-19 singles out Ananias) instructed Paul before baptizing him, they taught Paul this foundational creed.

This creed, which expresses the faith of the Church at its origin, emphasizes not only historical events but their Christian interpretations and their biblical explanations. The creed mentions first the fact that Christ died. Two statements based on faith then interpret the meaning of Jesus' death. The first is that Jesus died "for our sins": Although he was himself innocent, he was bruised for our offenses. The second provides biblical grounding and precedent for this faith statement, such as the song in Isaiah 52–53 about God's servant, who died taking on himself the punishment that the sins of others deserved.

This complex interrelationship of reported event and interpreting faith reveals how the very first Christians tried to understand and explain what happened to Jesus in the shocking event of his crucifixion. As Christians reflected on Jesus' death on the cross, they interpreted it as an undeserved death by an innocent sufferer. With the help of passages like

Isaiah 52–53, they realized that the reason Jesus had to suffer such a horrible death was that he was dying in our place and on our behalf, in order to take on himself the punishment that our sins deserved.

The next verifiable historical event mentioned in this primitive creed is that Jesus was buried (all four Gospels identify his tomb as belonging to Joseph of Arimathea). The subsequent claim in the creed is that Jesus was raised from the dead, which is essentially a faith statement that transcends the possibility of strict historical proof. The supplemental claim that Jesus was raised "on the third day" seems to follow directly and logically from the mention that he was buried. For according to all four Gospels his tomb was discovered empty on Sunday morning, the "third day" after his death and burial before sunset Friday evening.

According to the Gospels, Jesus died and was buried on Friday (the first day), before the beginning of the Sabbath observance at sundown Friday. He presumably lay in the tomb during Saturday, the Sabbath (and second day), during which the law did not allow his followers to work on his corpse. On Sunday (the third day), immediately after first light, women who went to provide further anointing of Jesus' corpse reported that the tomb was empty. At least Peter among the Twelve confirmed the women's report.

The further claim that all this took place "according to the scriptures" implies the results of a search of the Scriptures by the earliest believers to help them comprehend what the empty tomb might mean in relation to Jesus' being raised from the dead. For example, Luke 24:46 states: "Thus it is written, that the Christ should suffer and on the third day rise from the dead" (see also Luke 9:22 and Matthew 16:21). Many see in this quotation an implied reference to Hosea 6:2: "After two days he will revive us; on the third day he will raise us up, that we may live before him."

The next major section of this earliest Christian creed

refers to the second principal piece of evidence from which the apostles and the earliest Church argued that Jesus was raised from the dead—his appearances to named ("official?") witnesses. Thus the creed continues:

> He appeared to Cephas, then to the twelve. Then he appeared to more than five hundred brethren at one time, most of whom are still alive, though some have fallen asleep. Then he appeared to James, then to all the apostles.
>
> 1 CORINTHIANS 15:5-7

This early creed names Cephas or Peter as the first "official" witness. (Jesus seems to have appeared before this to Mary Magdalene, as mentioned in an ending later added at Mark 16:9: "Now when he rose early on the first day of the week, he appeared first to Mary Magdalene" [see Matthew 28:9-10; John 20:14-18]). The creed names as the second group of witnesses the Twelve, the official title for the inner circle, even though in the absence of Judas there remained at the time only eleven, including Peter.

This creed is the only documentation about the next major group of witnesses: "Then he appeared to more than five hundred brethren at one time, most of whom are still alive, though some have fallen asleep" (1 Corinthians 15:6). This group of five hundred witnesses is important for Paul's argument for two reasons. First, its large number makes it less open to charges of hallucination than an individual or small group would be. Second, Paul's emphasis that some are still alive implies, "If you don't believe me, you can ask some of them."

The last two witnesses named in the creed (whose list seems to be in at least roughly chronological order) are James, the future head of the church at Jerusalem (see Acts 15:13), and a group more inclusive than the Twelve whom Paul calls "apostles" (see 1 Corinthians 15:7). Here apostles apparently refers to other "official" witnesses besides the

Twelve, though in non-Pauline New Testament passages the term apostles is often synonymous with the Twelve. We know that in several letters Paul insists that he too is an apostle, even though he is obviously not one of the Twelve nor even among the witnesses who personally knew Jesus either in his ministry or in an appearance immediately following his resurrection.

At the end of this list of witnesses to a post-resurrection appearance of Jesus, Paul names himself as an admitted latecomer. But he insists that he is nevertheless a zealous witness and, as a matter of fact, a member of the same roster of apostles:

> Last of all, as to one untimely born, he appeared also to me. For I am the least of the apostles, unfit to be called an apostle, because I persecuted the church of God. But by the grace of God I am what I am, and his grace toward me was not in vain. On the contrary, I worked harder than any of them, though it was not I, but the grace of God which is with me. Whether then it was I or they, so we preach and so you believed.

1 CORINTHIANS 15:8-11

From Jesus' Resurrection to the Resurrection of All

Appealing to this traditional creed that they all accepted, in 1 Corinthians 15:12-19 Paul challenges the Corinthians to be consistent. How can anyone both accept the preaching that Christ is raised from the dead and also claim that there is no resurrection from the dead? "But if there is no resurrection of the dead, then Christ has not been raised" (1 Corinthians 15:13).

In addition, if Christ were not raised, Paul's preaching would be in vain and their faith would be in vain. Christians would still be in their sins, those who died in Christ would have perished without hope, and believers who hope in Christ would be the most to be pitied. "But in fact Christ has been raised from the dead, the first fruits of those who have fallen asleep" (15:20). The agricultural reference to "first fruits" implies that the rest of the harvest will follow. That is, Christians will be raised too.

Paul compares the way in which Christ is the cause of our resurrection with the way in which Adam caused the deaths of his descendants: "For as by a man came death, by a man has come also the resurrection of the dead. For as in Adam all die, so also in Christ shall all be made alive" (1 Corinthians 15:21-22). What happened to Jesus when he was raised from the dead will happen to the rest of us when Jesus returns in his parousia: "But each in his own order: Christ the first fruits, then at his coming those who belong to Christ" (15:23). Paul is here returning to the very bedrock of Christian belief: that Christ has indeed been raised from the dead. He uses that foundational doctrine to argue that Christ's resurrection is the first of many bodily resurrections, with special focus on the resurrection of Christians who have died.

Paul is also clear about the timing of this bodily resurrection of Christians. He confirms the Christian expectation that it will take place at Jesus' return at the end of time: "Then comes the end, when he delivers the kingdom to God the Father after destroying every rule and every authority and power" (1 Corinthians 15:24). As "in the beginning" Adam was given dominion over the earth, so in the new age Christ will have dominion over the kingdom and will thoroughly vanquish all God's enemies. Finally, at the very end, Christ in turn will hand over his kingdom to God his Father. "When all things are subjected to him, then the Son himself will also be subjected to him who put all things under him, that God may be everything to every one" (15:28).

Paul's scenario for the end times is thus quite vivid. At Christ's coming all who are "in Christ" shall be brought back to life. Christ the new Adam will completely overcome all

God's enemies and all resistance, ultimately even death. "Then comes the end," when Christ will hand over the kingdom to God the Father, so that God will be all in all.

To justify his expectation about the end of time, Paul has to overcome strong Greek skepticism at Corinth about how or even why bodily resurrection is important for the end times. He clearly rejects a crude notion of resurrection that would amount merely to resuscitation or restoration of our bodies to their present condition, still mortal and perishable. He makes it clear that the resurrected body will be as different from our present bodies as a plant is from its seed.

If someone gave you a black seed without telling you what kind of seed it was, you could not predict what it would look like after it was transformed into a plant. In the same way, our present body will be utterly transformed into a spiritualized body, whose shape is impossible to predict and which is no longer corruptible and mortal (see 1 Corinthians 15:35-38). "So is it with the resurrection of the dead. What is sown is perishable, what is raised is imperishable.... It is sown a physical body, it is raised a spiritual body" (15:42, 44). As we have borne the image of the man of dust, the first Adam, we shall also bear the image of the man of heaven, the last Adam, who is a life-giving spirit (see 15:45-49).

The key to Paul's insistence that our resurrected body will be spiritually transformed is the basic principle that "flesh and blood cannot inherit the kingdom of God, nor does the perishable inherit the imperishable" (1 Corinthians 15:50). Therefore Paul announces that he will reveal to his readers a mystery, a revelation:

> We shall not all sleep, but we shall all be changed, in a moment, in the twinkling of an eye, at the last trumpet. For the trumpet will sound, and the dead will be raised imperishable, and we shall be changed.
>
> 1 CORINTHIANS 15:51-52

Here Paul repeats his conviction that some Christians ("we") who happen to be alive when Jesus returns will not have to die to be transformed. "At the last trumpet," that is, at the public signal that "time is up," two things will happen. Christians who have died will be raised with imperishable bodies, and Christians still alive will have their bodies transformed so that they likewise will have immortal bodies. Neither group will be disadvantaged compared to the other. The basic principle is true for both: "For this perishable nature must put on the imperishable, and this mortal nature must put on immortality" (1 Corinthians 15:53).

In contrast to some theories of the rapture, Paul envisages that both the resurrection of the dead and the transformation of those who are still alive will occur at the very end of time, at the "final trumpet." These are not two temporally distinct events. This transformation of both those living and those dead at the "final trumpet" will be the definitive victory over death, which has oppressed humans throughout history. "When the perishable puts on the imperishable, and the mortal puts on immortality, then shall come to pass the saying that is written: 'Death is swallowed up in victory'" (1 Corinthians 15:54).

End Times Scenarios in the Letters to the Thessalonians

In the letter that scholars consider Paul's earliest, 1 Thessalonians, he already has to reassure Christians in a manner that is similar to the reassurance he will later give the Corinthians. He promises the Thessalonians, a group of Macedonian Christians influenced by Greek worldviews, that they need not grieve over fellow Christians who die before Christ's return at the end of the world. Paul assures them, "But we would not have you ignorant, brethren, concerning those who are asleep, that you may not grieve as others do who have no hope" (1 Thessalonians 4:13).

A huge difference between Christians and most pagans

(from whose ranks the Thessalonian community converted) is Christian hope as opposed to pagan despair in the face of death.[1] Paul argues that because God raised Jesus from the dead, he will also raise with Jesus those Christians who have died before his return (or parousia). Therefore those who have died have not lost their opportunity to share in the final victory of Christ's return but will participate in it equally with Christians who happen to be still alive at the end (1 Thessalonians 4:13-15).

To explain how this is possible, Paul repeats the scenario of the end times as he expects it to happen. Using conventional apocalyptic expressions from the Old Testament and other Jewish writings, as well as from common Christian traditions, some of which probably go back to Jesus, Paul portrays the Lord returning from heaven "with a cry of command, with the archangel's call, and with the sound of the trumpet of God" (1 Thessalonians 4:16). These biblical expressions (especially *the archangel's call* and *the sound of the trumpet of God*) provide the context for the following verse, which is often used to support theories of a rapture. It is true that verse 17 says that "we who are alive, who are left, shall be caught up together with them"—that is, with the newly resurrected Christians. However, verse 16 unquestionably refers to Jesus' public return as Judge at the end of the world, not to some earlier secret return of Jesus for a rapture of Christians before the tribulations.

In other words, Paul envisions the following end time occurrences: In his return the Lord descends from heaven "with the sound of the trumpet of God"—that is, publicly. The dead in Christ rise at his return. Then comes the parallel event: Believers who are still alive are "caught up together with them in the clouds to meet the Lord in the air." At this point all life on earth will have clearly come to an end, and both resurrected and transfigured Christians will be on their way to heaven with Jesus.

This passage cannot therefore be used as evidence for a rescue of Christians (by their being "raptured" into heaven) from the end time tribulations that the rest of humanity will yet have to suffer. The comfort offered is not that Christians can escape the sufferings expected in the tribulation, but rather that, at the end of time, faithful Christians, whether they die before the end of the world or not, will be taken up to heaven with the risen Jesus.

The Time of Jesus' Return

Paul then addresses questions about when Jesus will return. He refers to the teaching of Jesus himself that "the day of the Lord will come like a thief in the night" (1 Thessalonians 5:2; see Mark 13:33-37). God has not revealed the answer to the question of when Jesus will return, only that his return will be unpredictable. We are not meant to know the time beforehand. In fact, in Matthew 24:36, Jesus insists, "Of that day and hour no one knows, not even the angels of heaven, nor the Son, but the Father only" (see Acts 1:7).

After deflecting questions about "the times and the seasons" by comparing the coming of the Day of the Lord to that of a thief in the night (1 Thessalonians 5:1-22), Paul goes on to warn against the Thessalonians' being caught off guard. Sounding like the prophet Jeremiah, who complained about people "saying, 'Peace, peace,' when there is no peace" (Jeremiah 6:14), Paul warns, "When people say, 'There is peace and security,' then sudden destruction will come upon them as travail comes upon a woman with child, and there will be no escape" (1 Thessalonians 5:3).

Paul further urges his readers to remember that they are people who live in the light of day, not in the darkness of night, when people get drunk and do not stay awake (see 1 Thessalonians 5:4-7). He exhorts them to remain awake and sober and to be ready and armed for spiritual battle with the armor of faith, love, and hope (5:6, 8). "For God has not destined us for wrath, but to obtain salvation through our Lord Jesus Christ, who died for us so that whether we wake or sleep we might live with him" (5:9-10). Therefore Christians are to continue to encourage and build one another up (see 1 Thessalonians 5:11).

Paul's encouragement and consolation to the Thessalonians again comes not from a promise that Christ will snatch them to heaven and spare them the end time tribulations. He holds up the Christian hope that no matter what they suffer or whether they happen to be alive or dead when Jesus returns, the God who raised Jesus will also raise them to an unending life of happiness. They do not need to know when Jesus will return or what the scenario will be. They need only be ready at all times to meet Jesus as their Judge and Savior.

Corrected Perspectives

Although some scholars doubt that Paul wrote 2 Thessalonians, good arguments can be made for the traditional view that Paul wrote both letters within a relatively brief time span, the second letter responding to problems discovered after he had written the first.[2] Furthermore, all books in the Bible share fully the authority as God's revelation. We are not doing a historical investigation of Paul's personal views about the end times, but we are consulting 1 and 2 Thessalonians, as books in the canonical Bible, in our search for the prevalent biblical teaching about those times. Therefore we need not concern ourselves further with such historical questions. As the two letters have come down to us and been read within the canon, they clearly have the appearance of being successive responses to similar concerns, especially about what the end will be like and when it will take place. Therefore we can appropriately consult them in this canonical setting as related components of canonical biblical teaching about the end times.

Probably the main reason 2 Thessalonians was written was to respond to confusion and questions remaining after 1 Thessalonians about the coming of the Lord at the end of time. After the letter's introduction, 2 Thessalonians 2:1-12 corrects mistaken beliefs about the timing of Jesus' return. Paul must first assure his readers that the Day of the Lord has not already come, as some of them apparently fear. Perhaps this notion arose because of the persecutions and afflictions which they were suffering (2 Thessalonians 1:4-7).

Apostasy and the "Man of Lawlessness"

To reinforce his denial that the Day of the Lord has already come, Paul insists that two events must occur before that day: the rebellion or apostasy and the revelation or appearance of the "man of lawlessness," "the son of perdition" (2 Thessalonians 2:3). The relation between these two occurrences and their relative timing is not clear. One possibility is that they might both happen about the same time or even be referring to the same complex of events.

Paul describes the lawless one as "the son of perdition, who opposes and exalts himself against every so-called god or object of worship, so that he takes his seat in the temple of God, proclaiming himself to be God" (2 Thessalonians 2:3b-4). This portrayal calls to mind the biblical model of the arrogant Greek emperor and persecutor of the Jews, Antiochus IV, at the time of the Maccabean revolution. He placed the "abomination of desolation" in the temple (Daniel 11:31; 12:11, my translation) and referred to himself as "Epiphanes" or "the Appearance of God." The verse may also refer to the threat during Paul's lifetime that the Roman emperor Caligula might place a statue of himself (as a god to be worshipped) in the Jewish temple.[3]

Paul insists that the "mystery of lawlessness is already at work" (2 Thessalonians 2:7). Further, "you know what is restraining him now so that he may be revealed in his time"

(2:6). Although the first readers apparently knew to what or whom Paul was referring, contemporary readers and scholars do not. However, we do know that Paul suffered much in his ministry from abuse by mobs in conditions of political anarchy, and that he was repeatedly rescued by Roman authorities who suppressed the anarchy and restored order (see Acts 23:10). From this perspective, it might have been the Roman Empire or its local magistrates who were restraining the appearance of the man of lawlessness. But this restraint could not be expected to last indefinitely, and the Roman rulers could themselves sometimes act as lawless persecutors of Christians.

When Roman protection ceased, rebellion and "the lawless one" would be able to make their presence felt. Paul himself was to die about A.D. 64 during the unjust persecution of Christians by the Emperor Nero. In hindsight, we can see that Nero's persecution or his historical appearance as that particular "lawless one" was not connected with the end of the world. Almost every age, and certainly our own, can claim with justification to be a "time of apostasy," and every age has its "lawless ones." And the end is yet to come.

Paul assures his readers that when the lawless one is finally revealed at the end of time, his appearance will be shortened drastically because the Lord Jesus (at his own return and appearance) will destroy him (see 2 Thessalonians 2:8). This is not to downplay the great delusion that this one, reinforced by Satan and his pseudo-signs, will play upon many:

> The coming of the lawless one by the activity of Satan will be with all power and with pretended signs and wonders, and with all wicked deception for those who are to perish, because they refused to love the truth and so be saved. Therefore God sends upon them a strong delusion, to make them believe what is false, so that all may be

> condemned who did not believe the truth but had pleas-
> ure in unrighteousness.
>
> 2 THESSALONIANS 2:9-12

Implied in these comments is a strong warning and exhortation to Paul's readers to be ready not only for Jesus' return
in judgment but also for the preceding temptations of
deceivers strengthened by Satan's power.

The two letters to the Thessalonians provide compelling
examples of how difficult it is to describe a future end of the
world and the return of Jesus. In these letters God has
clearly underscored his revelation that there will be a judgment at the end of time. What is equally clear in both letters is that we do not know when Jesus will return. The
signs of his return are simply not distinctive enough and can
apply to too many plausible situations to make possible
unambiguous predictions about when the end will be.
Everyone must be ready for the final judgment at any time.

Conclusion

The Pauline letters of the New Testament clearly contrast
the damage done by Adam and the restoration by Jesus, the
new Adam. As the original man grasped at being as God and
thus lost his friendship with God and much of his dominion
over nature, so Christ emptied himself to take on the form
of a slave. To repair Adam's disobedience, the second Adam
was "obedient unto death, even death on a cross"
(Philippians 2:8). God therefore exalted him (initially
through resurrection from the dead) to become universally
acknowledged as Lord (see Philippians 2:5-11).

This final recognition of Jesus' universal dominion and
lordship will take place only in the end times, and human
participation in those end times will be primarily through
our also being raised from the dead. Therefore Paul's letters
explaining resurrection and recounting conventional end

time scenarios have provided valuable insight for some pre-liminary answers to our question "What does the Bible say about the end times?" It is now time to turn to the biblical book most exclusively focused on those times, the Book of Revelation or the Apocalypse.

Notes:

1. F.F. Bruce, "1 and 2 Thessalonians" in *Word Biblical Commentary*, Vol. 45 (Waco, Texas: Word, 1982), 95-97.

2. Bruce, xxxii-xlvi.

3. See Bruce, 168.

The End Times in Revelation

When most people hear the question "What does the Bible say about the end times?" the first book they think of consulting is the Book of Revelation, the Apocalypse. Yet only now in our last chapter are we turning to Revelation. For the Apocalypse is so thoroughly grounded in the rest of Scripture that the perspective of the rest of the Bible is needed to understand and appreciate its imagery and message.

Even Revelation itself hints at the necessity of reading that book in light of previous Scripture. First, the text of Revelation is virtually a mosaic of Old Testament symbols and phrases by which the seer John reports his own visions and messages from God. On American "Bible Belt" radio one can hear preachers speaking essentially in "King James English." Similarly, the Book of Revelation sounds as if it were written in Old Testament Greek.

Secondly, the way God identifies himself in the vision introducing Revelation suggests that the organizing perspective of Revelation is a comparison of the end time to primeval time, which is similar to the structure of this book. Earlier chapters have discussed the relationship between Endzeit (the end time) and Urzeit (the beginning or primeval time)—specifically, the fact that apocalyptic visions portraying the end of the world and the new creation customarily refer back to God's original creation of the world. That is, apocalypses typically visualize the end of the world with symbols taken from the world's beginning or creation. Thus, Revelation describes a new creation at the end of the present world in terms that are reminiscent of the original creation as recounted in Genesis.

Interpreting Symbols

Before we begin a close reading of the text itself, we need to recall what kind of writing Revelation is. Revelation is an apocalyptic narration of visions and verbal messages mediated by divine or angelic messengers. For example, the passage in Revelation 20 about the millennium is not a creedal statement, a catechism summary of doctrine, nor even a dogmatic or theological statement. It narrates the contents of a vision John received.

I find it helpful when considering the symbolism of visions to consider the analogous symbolism of more commonly experienced dreams. As I find it unwise to try to over-interpret every detail of a dream, so am I reluctant to over-interpret every detail of visions, including those in Scripture.[1]

Paul seems to show such a reluctance concerning even his own visions:

> I know a man in Christ who fourteen years ago was caught up to the third heaven—whether in the body or out of the body I do not know, God knows. And I know that this man was caught up into Paradise—whether in the body or out of the body I do not know, God knows—and he heard things that cannot be told, which man may not utter.
>
> 2 CORINTHIANS 12:2-4

Many historical examples of arbitrary and irresponsible interpretation of the visions of Ezekiel, Daniel, and Revelation prove the wisdom of such reluctance.

The symbols in dreams and visions are more closely related to metaphors and analogies than they are to factual descriptions of realities. These symbols necessarily portray spiritual and abstract realities by means of concrete images that can (generally) be imagined. Therefore we begin by recalling that when the seer John writes, "Then I saw an angel coming down from heaven" (Revelation 20:1), or, "Then I saw thrones" (20:4), he is narrating visions that he had, with all the symbolism one expects in visions. He is not making a dogmatic or creedal statement predicting, for example, that there will be a historical thousand-year intermediate reign of Christ and his martyrs on earth before the final victory over Satan and evil, followed by the Last Judgment.

The different levels of meaning in apocalyptic writings like Revelation were virtually self-evident to first-century readers, who were used to this genre of writing. However, they are quite foreign to our cultural experience today. Perhaps an analogy to reading the Sunday newspaper can clarify the dynamics of interpretation.

Today, when American adults read the different sections of a Sunday newspaper, they instinctively shift gears in how they interpret the different kinds of writing within the single paper. They know that when they read news articles in the main section, they are reading narratives that implicitly claim to recount events (more or less) as they happened. When they get to the editorial page, they recognize that the writers are emphasizing their own opinions rather than reporting events—opinions with which the readers will tend either to agree or disagree. Readers also instinctively realize that stories in the comic section are primarily fictional and often intentionally humorous, not fact-based news reports. And when they read in the sports section that so-and-so "stole second base," they know that, in the context of baseball, this was a praiseworthy achievement, not a crime.

Likewise, apocalyptic writings use metaphors, jargon, and technical symbols and terms that were familiar to the originally intended readers but are foreign to contemporary cultural experience. Therefore we must take care not to interpret expressions in ancient apocalyptic jargon by only the literal dictionary meanings. Let us look closely at the descriptions of these visions with an awareness of the special meanings of many of the conventional apocalyptic expressions and try to understand their symbolic implications.

Revelation 1:8: God's Initial Self-Revelation

In Revelation 1:8 the very first self-revelation of God recalls the association between Revelation and Genesis: "'I am the Alpha and the Omega,' says the Lord God, 'who is and who was and who is to come, the Almighty.'" The Alpha, the beginning of the Greek alphabet, symbolizes the beginning of reality. As Scripture has taught, beginning with Genesis, God is the beginning, the source, the almighty Creator of everything out of nothing by his mere word of command.

The omega, the last letter of the Greek alphabet, conveys the fact that God is also the end and goal of all creation, not only its Creator and source. Human creatures are made by the Creator to be united in love with their Creator. "You have made us for yourself, O God, and our hearts are restless till they rest in you."[2] Whether or not human creatures achieve their final goal of union with their Creator depends on their own free responses to God's offers of love and grace and to his commandments. This accountability factor, therefore, includes within the symbol of God as Omega the concept of God as ultimate Judge.

The title "the one who is and who was and who is to come, the Almighty" implies that God has unlimited power and total dominion over history—present, past, and future. The self-introduction of God in this initial vision emphasizes that God has complete authority over world and human history, from the first moment in which as Alpha he created it (narrated in Genesis) until the end of time, when creatures will either definitively attain or miss their goal in God as Omega.

Yet Revelation 1:17-18 adds a new dimension to what was revealed about God in Genesis and echoed in Revelation 1:8 above. In Revelation 1:17-18 Jesus, appearing as the Son of Man, proclaims, "Fear not, I am the first and the last, and the living one; I died, and behold I am alive for evermore, and I have the keys of Death and Hades."

The "first and last" in Jesus' self-designation unmistakably echoes the "Alpha and Omega" by which God has just described himself. Verse 8 focuses on God as beginning and goal because he is the all-powerful Lord of history (past, present, and future). He is Creator and goal and Judge of human creatures. The parallel focus on Jesus in verses 17-18 also emphasizes Jesus as first and last but from a different perspective. He is first and last because he is the resurrected living one, who died and now lives eternally, and who has completely conquered and now controls what will ultimately happen not only to death but also to Hades, the domain of the dead. Revelation 1:17-18 focuses on Jesus as the source of the new creation through his own resurrection and through his control over the keys of Death and Hades. These verses also point to Jesus' coming role as judge at the end of time.

Charles Talbert has maintained that the canonical Bible as a whole has one overarching theological plot concerning the world from its beginning to its ending: "Creation, Fall, Covenant, Christ, Church, Consummation." All of the Bible has to be read within this overall theological plot. The biblical plot begins with our ultimate origins in Creation (Genesis 1–11) and ends with our ultimate destiny in the New Creation (in Revelation).[3]

Within the complete canon of the Bible, the Apocalypse or Revelation is positioned as the Bible's last book. Revelation gives God's final answer to the problem of evil, which has been lurking behind all the biblical writings, beginning with the Fall in Genesis 3. Genesis 3:15 provided some immediate if somewhat mysterious reassurance by God that he would repair this disaster of human disobedience and alienation from their Creator: "I will put enmity between you [the serpent] and the woman, and between your seed and her seed; he shall bruise your head, and you shall bruise his heel." Thus the very first book of Scripture assures its readers that a descendant of the woman, who is the "mother of all living" (Genesis 3:20), will ultimately crush the Satan figure who has contributed so significantly to humans' alienation from God. The vision in Revelation 12 of the messianic son of the woman and Satan's expulsion from heaven seems clearly to relate back to this primeval promise.

We have seen in the Pauline letters, especially Philippians 2, God's fulfillment of this promise and his answer to the self-promoting pride of Adam's striving to be as God. To counter human self-promotion, the Son of God emptied himself, first to become man. He then emptied himself further to obey God even unto death on a cross (see Philippians 2:6-8). Although Jesus himself was promptly vindicated by his resurrection and exaltation as Lord in heaven (2:9-11), this vindication has yet to be fully and publicly accomplished and recognized in human history and its culmination. Evil continues to inflict immense damage on the world and especially on the Church. In human history as we know it, we are not likely to witness "that at the name of Jesus every knee should bow, in heaven and on earth and under the earth, and every tongue confess that Jesus Christ is Lord, to the glory of God the Father" (Philippians 2:10-11).

Revelation is an entire book dedicated to revealing and emphasizing God's ultimate victory over sin and death and Satan, no matter how much evil now seems to be prevailing. In the prophecies and visions of the seer John, God reveals his heavenly plan for completing his repair of the damage done by human sin and for saving those who have been victimized by sin (their own or those of others). God reveals how he plans to overthrow and punish both oppressors and unrepentant sinners and to restore justice to the universe, which he created good but which humans and evil spirits have sabotaged. In the many visions and prophecies of Revelation, God provides a multifaceted and vivid set of responses to the problems of evil and death, which have acted as backdrop for the many dramas of sin and salvation throughout both the Old and New Testaments.

The Visionary of Revelation

Most apocalypses use a conventional fiction of pseudonymous authorship—that is, writing under the name of some seer or holy person from the ancient past. Thus, there are Jewish apocalypses attributed to Adam, to Abraham, and to Enoch.

The intriguing figure of Enoch was used for several non-biblical apocalyptic works that still survive. Enoch is the seventh in the genealogical line from Adam: Adam to Seth to Enosh to Kenan to Mahalalel to Jared to Enoch. The genealogy mentions how each of the others lived some nine hundred-plus years and then died. For example, "Thus all the days of Jared were nine hundred and sixty-two years; and he died" (Genesis 5:20). In sharp contrast, "all the days of Enoch were three hundred and sixty-five years. Enoch walked with God; and he was not, for God took him" (5:23-24).

Because Enoch "walked with God," and because God took him well before the age of the deaths of the others and without any mention of his dying, Jewish and biblical traditions considered that Enoch was taken up into heaven without dying—as was Elijah. (This may have affected Paul's envisaging how those still alive at Jesus' return will have their bodies transformed to become immortal [see 1 Thessalonians 4:15-17 and 1 Corinthians 15:49-53]). *Enoch* thus became a favorite name used by later apocalyptic seers who wanted to describe visionary trips to heaven (similar to New Testament visions described in Revelation 4–5 and 2 Corinthians 12:2-4).

However, just as Paul provides a frankly autobiographic account of his own visionary experience in 2 Corinthians 12, this Christian apocalypse, Revelation, forthrightly identifies its actual author. "I John, your brother, who share with you in Jesus the tribulation and the kingdom and the patient endurance, was on the island called Patmos on account of the word of God and the testimony of Jesus" (Revelation 1:9). The person who received the visions that he is about to narrate identifies himself simply by his name John, a common Jewish and Christian name. Whereas the intended readers were expected to know which John this is, later readers who are no longer from that age and context cannot be as certain.

Unlike Paul, who consistently and emphatically refers to himself as an apostle or servant of God (a term Old Testament prophets regularly used of themselves), the visionary of the Apocalypse calls himself simply "John, your brother." He expands on this by referring to himself as sharing in Jesus with the recipients of this book in "the tribulation and the kingdom and the patient endurance." "Tribulation" translates the Greek word *thlipsis*, which is regularly used in apocalyptic passages to describe the sufferings of the end times (see Mark 13:19; Matthew 24:21; Revelation 7:14). It is used elsewhere in the New Testament to describe especially persecution for one's faith (see Acts 11:19; 14:22) or for or with Christ (Romans 5:3, Colossians 1:24). In general, New Testament writings expect Christians to have to undergo tribulation from hostile elements in the world as a consequence of their faith in Christ. Revelation is no exception.

The author John unquestionably has an authority that is recognized by the churches in Asia to whom he writes, for he expects them to heed the prophetic messages he sends to the "seven churches." However, the authority he claims here is not that of an apostle or church founder, such as Paul regularly claimed for himself in his letters. The authority John asserts is that of a prophet to whom God's word has been directly revealed in visions and prophecies and who is now passing on that "word of the Lord" to God's people, as the Old Testament prophets also did.

John explains that he was exiled to the Roman penal colony on this barren island "on account of the word of God and the testimony of Jesus" (Revelation 1:9b). In other words, he had been preaching the Christian message and bearing witness to Jesus. The punishment by exile—rather than by more easily carried out punishments such as imprisonment, beating, or execution—seems to imply that Roman authorities recognized in John a social status above that of a mere foreigner or slave.

The Initial Vision

This prophet John explains the circumstances under which he received this inaugural vision: "I was in the Spirit on the Lord's day" (Revelation 1:10). This sentence indicates that when John heard the loud voice like a trumpet on Sunday, the Lord's Day for Christians, he was swept up in prayer. (Perhaps a reason why he was praying on that day was his desire to be united from his lonely exile on the island of Patmos with the Sunday worship of Christians on the mainland.)

John heard in his prayer "a loud voice like a trumpet saying, 'Write what you see in a book and send it to the seven churches'" (Revelation 1:10-11). The various individual elements in this initial vision, which is what John saw when he turned to look at the speaker, will reappear among the seven messages to the churches. In the midst of seven golden lampstands John saw "one like a son of man, clothed with a long robe and with a golden girdle round his breast; his head and his hair were white as white wool, white as snow; his eyes were like a flame of fire...and his face was like the sun shining in full strength" (1:13-14, 16).

Daniel 7 emphasized differences between the Son of Man and the Ancient of Days before whose heavenly throne he presented himself (though Greek translations of Daniel tend to combine their attributes). In contrast, John's description of the risen Christ as one like a Son of Man is more like Daniel 7's portrayal of the divine Ancient of Days. Both have dazzling white hair and flaming eyes and a face shining like the sun,[4] symbols of divinity.

Other scriptural symbols of divine authority pervade John's vision of the "one like a son of man": "His voice was like the sound of many waters; in his right hand he held seven stars, from his mouth issued a sharp two-edged sword" (Revelation 1:15-16). The voice that sounded like the roar of many waters recalls Old Testament prophetic references to God or to God's angelic messengers. Holding stars of heaven in one's hand would ordinarily imply divinity. Although the image of a two-edged sword coming from someone's mouth is only found in Revelation, it can imply a sense of a spoken judgment or a stated differentiation between good and evil, which the Old Testament frequently attributes to God.

When John falls at the feet of the person in this vision, as is customary in Old Testament appearances of God, the one like a Son of Man gives the usual Old Testament reassurance, "Fear not" (Revelation 1:17b). However, this encounter differs starkly from many biblical angelic appearances, in which the angel tells the seer not to worship a fellow creature. It is unlike even the later encounter in Revelation 19:10: "Then I fell down at his feet to worship...but he said to me, 'You must not do that! I am a fellow servant with you and your brethren who hold the testimony of Jesus. Worship God.'"

Here in Revelation 1:17, the exhortation not to fear is followed by words that might be expected to make one's fear worse. "Fear not, I am the first and the last" (verse 17b) clearly echoes God's revelation of himself, "I am the Alpha and the Omega," in verse 8. However, the additional reference of Jesus to his resurrection refocuses attention on his humanity: "[I am] the living one; I died, and behold I am alive for evermore, and I have the keys of Death and Hades" (1:18). Possessing attributes that apply both to God and to man, Jesus also maintains that he has "the keys of Death and Hades." It is hard to imagine a more powerful claim to ultimate judgment of the fate of humans than the claim to have the keys of death and of Hades, the realm of death.

Letters to the Churches: Revelation 2–3

In Revelation 2–3 the Son of Man dictates to John messages in the form of letters to the seven churches of Asia. These messages provide a quasi-letter setting for the written visions and prophecies that make up the rest of Revelation. Although there is an urgency about Jesus' return in the background of all of these letters, they focus readers' attention not primarily on trying to determine the "times or seasons," nor on decoding the many symbols and visions, but on the endurance and fidelity that will be expected of all the churches in the coming times of tribulation.

The letters provide an atmosphere of exhortation, encouragement, and warning, according to the differing needs of the various church communities. Jesus will "give to each of you as your works deserve" (Revelation 2:23). The message to each of the seven churches contains the same final exhortation, "He who has an ear, let him hear what the Spirit says to the churches" (2:7, 11, 17, 29; 3:6, 13, 22).

These introductory messages contextualize within a serious moral and religious atmosphere all the symbols and visions and prophecies that follow, no matter how exotic some of the latter may appear. The letters invite an interpretation of the visions primarily in terms of religious and moral exhortation and encouragement. They indicate that the first-century writer does not primarily expect twenty-first–century readers to try to decode the symbols in order to figure out a blow-by-blow scenario of the end times.

Visions of the Heavenly Throne and the Lamb

In apocalyptic writings, a conventional way to introduce visions of heaven is to report a door opening in heaven for the seer to enter: "After this I looked, and lo, in heaven an open door! And the first voice, which I had heard speaking to me like a trumpet, said, 'Come up hither, and I will show you what must take place after this'" (Revelation 4:1). The seer's response makes it clear that this is a description of a vision, not an actual opening of a door in heaven, whatever that might even mean: "At once I was in the Spirit, and lo [literally 'behold' or 'look'], a throne stood in heaven, with one seated on the throne!" (4:2). As we saw in Revelation 1:10, the phrase "in the Spirit" refers to being in an intense state of prayer.

The seer does not try to describe God sitting on the throne, except by a passing comparison to precious jewels (see Revelation 4:3). He focuses instead on the heavenly setting: the rainbow around the throne, the twenty-four elders seated on twenty-four thrones around the central throne, the lightning, the seven torches of fire, and the sea of glass (see 4:4-6).

Also around the throne are four exotic living creatures (who, from the complexity of their descriptions, are actually difficult to imagine). They are full of eyes and look respectively like a lion, an ox, something with the face of a man, and a flying eagle. Each has six wings filled with eyes, and they sing without ceasing, "Holy, holy, holy, is the Lord God Almighty, who was and is and is to come!" (Revelation 4:8b; compare Isaiah 6:3). In describing this vision of God on his throne amid his heavenly council, the seer uses obvious details from heavenly visions that he has read in Isaiah 6 and Ezekiel 1.

Whenever the four living creatures give glory to God on the throne, the twenty-four elders cast their crowns before God's throne and prostrate themselves in worship. "Worthy art thou, our Lord and God, to receive glory and honor and power, for thou didst create all things, and by thy will they existed and were created" (Revelation 4:11). Whatever the four living creatures symbolize, they are treated as angelic beings in Ezekiel and probably also here. Their purpose seems primarily to praise and worship God on his throne. The twenty-four elders, who probably symbolize a combination of the twelve tribes of Israel and the twelve apostles (or possibly the twenty-four classes of Levitical priests in the temple worship), are evidently human figures.

This image powerfully portrays what should have happened in the beginning of human creation in Genesis. This heavenly worship reverses what went wrong when the first humans refused to worship and obey God but tried instead to "be as God" themselves. Whereas in the beginning God put humans in dominion over the rest of creation (for which crowns and thrones would be appropriate symbols), they tried to compete with God's own divine dominion. In effect, the first humans refused to "lay their crowns before God's throne."

Now in the end times, the twenty-four elders in this vision of heaven symbolize human religious authority finally submitting to God's authority. They do so not only as human beings who have dominion over lesser material creatures (as Adam and Eve did) but also as the heads of the twelve tribes of Israel with their Old Testament authority and as the twelve apostles with their New Testament authority. These human authority figures all lay their crowns before the throne of the Creator and worship prostrate before him. They reverse the rebellion of the first humans and finally fulfill the original purpose for which God created the human race.

The Lion and the Lamb

John then sees in God's hand "a scroll written within and on

149

the back, sealed with seven seals" (Revelation 5:1b). An angel asks, "Who is worthy to open the scroll and break its seals?" (5:2b). The seer weeps because no one is found worthy, until one of the elders tells him, "Weep not; lo, the Lion of the tribe of Judah, the Root of David, has conquered, so that he can open the scroll and its seven seals" (5:5b).

"The Lion of Judah from David" refers to Jesus as Davidic Messiah, but the symbolism in this vision is unexpected. John sees in his vision not a lion but "a Lamb standing, as though it had been slain" (Revelation 5:6b). The symbol of a lion is one of power. A lamb standing as though slain does not remotely connote power, but it rather symbolizes Jesus' being sacrificed (without resisting the injustice done to him) as the Passover Lamb to save his people and now standing resurrected and alive.

This startling symbol in John's vision is consistent with the surprise experienced by many of God's people Israel, who for centuries expected their promised Messiah to be a powerful liberator who would save them from their political oppressors. It was a Lion of Judah that they were anticipating; they were quite unprepared for a Lamb who would be slain. This clash of expectations is one more illustration of how prophetic fulfillment often differs radically from what people are expecting. Christian believers can recognize in hindsight the relevance of an Old Testament passage to Jesus. Contemporaries of Jesus did not have the benefit of this perspective.

The song about the suffering servant in Isaiah 53 provides an example of Revelation's symmetry of the Lion of Judah with the Lamb who was slain. This prophecy did not have significant influence on the expectations of many Jews about their coming Messiah, as they tended to imagine him rather as a second David who would conquer their oppressors. Christians were probably motivated to focus on this prophecy because they found in it some meaningful explanation for Jesus' suffering and death.

This illustrates how impossible it is and always has been for biblical believers to predict blow-by-blow scenarios for prophesied events. Hindsight reveals how difficult it was for Old Testament Jews to imagine what the prophesied messianic figure would be like. Why should we expect that it will be easier for us to imagine in detail what his second coming will be like? As God had to repeat on multiple occasions to his people, "My thoughts [even in prophecies], are not your thoughts, neither are your ways my ways, says the LORD" (Isaiah 55:8).

In both the Old and New Testaments, God's promises and predictions about the future, especially about the distant and therefore unimaginable future, are consistently worded in symbolic and even conventional expressions. The necessarily mysterious nature of such prophecies renders quite suspect contemporary attempts to extract from them a detailed scenario of the end times. These attempts are a staple of writings like the Left Behind books and of rapture theories.

The Lamb Takes the Scroll

Though no one else was found worthy to open the seals of the scroll, the Lamb without hesitation accepts it from God's right hand. The members of the heavenly court break into a new song of praise: "Worthy art thou to take the scroll and to open its seals, for thou wast slain and by thy blood didst ransom men for God from every tribe and tongue and people and nation, and hast made them a kingdom and priests to our God, and they shall reign on earth" (Revelation 5:9-10). The reason the Lamb is worthy to open the scroll is that by shedding his blood, he ransomed for God a new priestly and royal people.

The vision shows the heavenly council's continued praise of the Lamb, a praise that imitates their praise of God himself on the throne: "Worthy is the Lamb who was slain, to receive power and wealth and wisdom and might and honor and glory and blessing!" (Revelation 5:12). Every creature in heaven, on earth, under the earth, and in the sea joins in this heavenly song of praise, which they direct jointly to God on the throne and to the Lamb: "To him who sits upon the throne and to the Lamb be blessing and honor and glory and might for ever and ever!" (5:13b). The four living creatures respond, "Amen," and the twenty-four elders worship prostrate (5:14).

These songs of praise to the Lamb and to God on the throne are among the most powerful songs of praise in the New Testament. They also portray the heavenly court using almost identical terms of praise both for the One on the throne and for the Lamb. Such a parallel treatment of the Lamb with that of the One on the throne can legitimately be interpreted as a very exalted view of the Lamb—specifically, that the Lamb is divine.

The Seven Seals

The next set of visions observes the Lamb opening the seven seals. As he opens each seal, the four living creatures call, "Come." After the first seal, a rider on a white horse comes forth conquering with a bow; after the second, a rider on a red horse brings the slaughter of war to the earth; after the third seal, a rider on a black horse with a balance foreshadows famine; after the fourth, Death, riding a pale horse, and Hades are given power to kill a fourth of the earth by "sword and with famine and with pestilence and by wild beasts of the earth" (Revelation 6:8b).

When the Lamb opens the fifth seal, the souls of the martyrs cry out from under the altar, "O Sovereign Lord, holy and true, how long before thou wilt judge and avenge our blood on those who dwell upon the earth?" (Revelation 6:10b). They are told to be patient until the number of martyrs has been completed (see 6:11). In Revelation 20 these same souls will finally be given the special honor of reigning with Christ (see 20:4-6).

After the Lamb opens the sixth seal, "all heaven broke loose": a huge earthquake, the sun blackened, the moon like blood, stars falling to the earth, the sky vanishing, and every mountain and island moved from its foundation. These are characteristic apocalyptic symbols for cosmic signs at the end of the world. The kings and great ones hide in caves from the "face of him who is seated on the throne, and from the wrath of the Lamb" (Revelation 6:16).

The Sealing of the 144,000

Before the opening of the seventh seal, there is a dramatic pause. Prior to any more devastation, an angel commands other angels, "Do not harm the earth or the sea or the trees, till we have sealed the servants of our God upon their foreheads" (Revelation 7:3). This notion of a protective seal or mark on God's servants recalls the blood of the Passover lamb on the doorposts of the Israelites, sparing them from the angel who was to kill the firstborn of the Egyptians (see Exodus 12). It also alludes to Ezekiel 9:4, where the faithful Jews who grieved over the sins of the others were given a protective mark on their forehead before the six heavenly executioners slaughtered all the others without pity or exception.

The symbolic number of 144,000 who are marked for protection from the punishing plagues is divided into portions of 12,000, one portion for each of the tribes of the sons of Israel. Oddly, the tribe of Dan is omitted, perhaps because of its associations with idolatry (see Judges 18:30; 1 Kings 12:28-29). Manasseh, a son of Joseph, is listed in Dan's place.[5]

The seer goes on to describe an innumerable multitude from every nation standing before the throne and the Lamb and singing a song of praise for salvation. There have been debates over whether the 144,000 and this multitude are different groups or the same group under two different symbols or from two different perspectives. In Revelation 7 the first group, the 144,000, is unquestionably located on earth and being sealed for protection against the coming tribulation; later, in Revelation 14 the same 144,000 will appear in heaven before God's throne after they have "been redeemed from the earth" (Revelation 14:3b), presumably after enduring that tribulation.

The second group, in Revelation 7:9-17, is unmistakably located not on earth but in heaven, because they are standing before God's heavenly throne, clothed in the white robes of heaven with the palm branches of victory and praising God with the angels, living creatures, and entire court of heaven. In Revelation 7:14 they are explicitly identified: "These are they who have come out of the great tribulation; they have washed their robes and made them white in the blood of the Lamb." Because they have been faithful to the Lamb on earth, even in suffering, "therefore are they before the throne of God, and serve him day and night within his temple; and he who sits upon the throne will shelter them with his presence" (7:15).

Therefore, the most likely explanation of the 144,000 on earth and the innumerable multitude in heaven is that from different perspectives and under different symbols, they both represent the Church and its members: The 144,000 represent the Church on earth who will undergo the great tribulation, and the innumerable multitude symbolize the more inclusive number of the Church triumphant in heaven after they have come through and beyond that tribulation. In Revelation 14:4 the 144,000 are referred to as the "first fruits for God and the Lamb." The implication seems to be that after these "first fruits" will come the rest of those saved in heaven, to make up the innumerable multitude at the end of time.

In heaven the entire celestial court prostrate themselves before the throne and worship God: "Amen! Blessing and glory and wisdom and thanksgiving and honor and power and might be to our God for ever and ever! Amen"

(Revelation 7:12). One of the twenty-four elders explains to the seer that because this multitude has passed through the great tribulation in fidelity to the Lamb, they now serve before God's throne in the heavenly temple. The one on the throne "will shelter them with his presence. They shall hunger no more, neither thirst any more; the sun shall not strike them, nor any scorching heat" (7:15b-16). In a striking paradox the Lamb will be their shepherd and will guide them to living water; "and God will wipe away every tear from their eyes" (7:17b).

Seven Trumpets and Three Woes

The pacing of the opening of the seals suddenly slows, and tension is heightened when the Lamb finally opens the seventh seal. Ominously, there is "silence in heaven for about half an hour" (Revelation 8:1b). A new, spiraling series of seven trumpets begins, each bringing plagues reminiscent of those in Exodus (see Exodus 7-11). Neither the narration of the plagues in Exodus nor that in Revelation focuses on God's wrath or punishment for its own sake, but rather on divine efforts to save God's people or to elicit change or repentance from evildoers.

Before the fifth trumpet is blown, an eagle cries three woes on those who are alive on earth when the last three trumpets blow (see Revelation 8:13). The first of the three woes accompanies the fifth trumpet blast (9:12). John sees a star falling from heaven and opening the shaft of the bottomless pit, so that smoke arises from it and darkens the sun and air (9:1-2). Out of this smoke come locusts with the power and sting of scorpions to attack the earth, but not green vegetation or trees nor those humans who have God's seal on their foreheads (9:3-4). For five months they torture with stings like a scorpion's the humans who lack God's seal but do not kill them, though many long to die (9:5-6).

The second woe comes at the sound of the sixth trumpet. Four angels who have been bound till "the hour, the day, the month, and the year" are released to kill a third of the human race (Revelation 9:13-15). John sees a huge number of cavalry whose horses have lions' heads, which are breathing fire, smoke, and sulphur, and they inflict pain by their serpent-like tails (9:16-19). Despite God's punishments, those humans not killed by these plagues continue to refuse to repent of their sinful deeds or to stop worshiping demons and idols that cannot "see or hear or walk" (see 9:20). "[N]or did they repent of their murders or their sorceries or their immorality or their thefts" (9:21).

Before the third woe and the seventh and final trumpet blast, there is another pause in the action. John sees a mighty angel holding open a little scroll in his hand and shouting loudly so that seven thunders sound (see 10:1-3). John is commanded not to write what the seven thunders said but to seal it up (see Revelation 10:4). This contrasts sharply with all the previous instructions to write down everything he sees and hears in visions. Then a huge angel swears by God almighty that there should be no more delay, but when the seventh trumpet is sounded, "the mystery of God, as he announced to his servants the prophets, should be fulfilled" (10:7b).

This vision about eating a small scroll recalls a similar vision in Ezekiel 2:8–3:3 and underlines the seer's continuity with the Old Testament prophets and the similarity between his call and message and theirs. Perhaps the symbolism of eating the scroll suggests that the prophet makes his message fully his own. The contrast between sweetness and bitterness might be related to the "good news-bad news" nature of the prophetic message. Ultimately, there will be victory, but it will come through suffering, from which the prophet himself will not be fully spared.

Just as Revelation begins with a scene recounting the call of John to prophesy (see Revelation 1:9-20), so here in the second half of Revelation comes another commission: "You must again prophesy about many peoples and nations and tongues and kings" (10:11). John is instructed to perform a prophetic and symbolic action: to take a measuring rod and measure the temple of God and its altar. He is not, however, to measure the court outside, for that is given over to the nations who will trample the city for the same symbolic period of forty-two months (three and a half years or 1,260 days, see Revelation 11:1-2). John then prophesies about two witnesses who will prophesy in sackcloth for the same period of 1,260 days (11:3).

These two prophets are Zechariah's two olive trees standing by the lampstands (see Zechariah 4:3, 11, 14). They have much in common with the Old Testament prophets Moses and Elijah. Fire coming from heaven to devour those who would harm them is reminiscent of Elijah (see 2 Kings 1:10), as is the power to prevent rain from falling (see 1 Kings 17:1). The power to turn water into blood recalls the signs that were worked through Moses to pressure the pharaoh to release God's people (see Exodus 7:17, 19-20).

When the prophets have finished their testimony, the beast from the bottomless pit will conquer and kill them and leave their dead bodies to rot "in the street of the great city which is allegorically called Sodom and Egypt, where their Lord was crucified" (Revelation 11:8). The reference to Jesus' crucifixion seems to apply the allegorical "Sodom" and "Egypt" to Jerusalem, although those symbols usually refer to Rome. Unlike Jesus, who rose on the third day, the corpses of these prophets will be mocked unburied for three and a half days.

Also, unlike Jesus' resurrection, which was not witnessed by any of his enemies, these Christian prophets are resurrected after three and a half days in the sight of many, who are overcome with great fear (see Revelation 11:9-11).

In the sight of their foes they are summoned and raised up to heaven (Revelation 11:12), as was Elijah, but he in the sight of his disciple. At the ascension of the two prophets, a great earthquake topples a tenth of the city of Jerusalem and kills seven thousand people (a symbolic number), while the majority of the city's inhabitants in their terror give glory to God (see 11:13).

The Announcement of God's Salvation

Many scholars consider Revelation 11:15–12:17 a major turning point in the Book of Revelation. At least in anticipation, these visions portray God's final victory over evil, especially as personified by the dragon or Satan. From another perspective, the defeat of Satan will be again portrayed in Revelation 20, where Satan is bound for a thousand years, while the souls of the martyrs reign with Christ, and then loosed one last time to lead an absolutely final and futile battle against God's reign.

The action begins when the seventh angel finally blows his trumpet. Heavenly voices announce God's salvation: "The kingdom of the world has become the kingdom of our Lord and of his Christ, and he shall reign for ever and ever" (Revelation 11:15b). The twenty-four elders prostrate themselves and worship God with a song of praise that God has finally "taken thy great power and begun to reign" (11:17b). Though the nations have been raging against God for millennia (this is pretty much the entire biblical story line), God's wrath and punishment have only now finally come upon them, as well as the time for the ultimate, definitive judgment of all humans.

This "Last Judgment" will lead to "rewarding thy servants, the prophets and saints, and those who fear thy name, both small and great, and…destroying the destroyers of the earth" (Revelation 11:18). This song celebrates a vindication of God's reign that actually has not yet been narrated in the text, and thus it functions somewhat as a preview of what is to come. The next thing seen in John's vision is God's temple in heaven opened, exposing the ark of the covenant within. The usual apocalyptic "fireworks" of "lightning, voices, peals of thunder, an earthquake, and heavy hail" accompany this (11:19).

The Woman and the Dragon

John next narrates two mutually antagonistic signs or portents that he sees in heaven: "a woman clothed with the sun" and "a great red dragon" (Revelation 12:1, 3). These visions symbolize much of the biblical history of human rebellion against God and the messiah Jesus' victory over it. The woman clothed with the sun is one of my favorite biblical symbols. It has at least three levels (or changing applications) of meaning. These different levels should not surprise us when we recall that these are visions, the symbolism of which is comparable to the more commonly experienced symbolism in dreams. There a symbol often changes in mid-dream. A beneficial symbol can suddenly become threatening, or one person in the dream can be replaced by another with no warning or explanation.

The immediate referent for the symbol of the woman giving birth to the messianic son, who escapes the devil-dragon's jaws by being swept up to God's throne, is not the birth of the Messiah but his death and resurrection. Thus, at this point in the vision, the woman is most immediately related to God's Old Testament people, who produced the Messiah. However, when the dragon goes "to make war on the rest of her offspring, on those who keep the commandments of God and bear testimony to Jesus" (Revelation 12:17), the woman clearly has come to refer to the Church. On a third level, and based on the wording of the passage itself, most Christians have also seen in this woman allusions to Mary, the actual mother of Jesus the Messiah.

A symbolic merging between the Church and Mary is not unique to Revelation 12. The Gospel of John coalesces in a similar manner the symbols and functions of Mary and the Church. On the cross the dying Jesus gives his mother (symbolically applicable to both Mary and the Church) to his beloved disciple (both John and "every Christian" or member of the Church) to be his mother (see John 19:26-27).

The Fall of the Accuser

When the messianic son is snatched away from the dragon and taken up to God in heaven (see Revelation 12:5), a war arises there, and Michael and his angels expel from heaven the dragon and his angels (see 12:7-9). The victory song that follows provides a principal key to the meaning of Revelation. It provides both the "good news" and "bad news" at the heart of Revelation. The good news is "Now the salvation and the power and the kingdom of our God and the authority of his Christ have come, for the accuser of our brethren has been thrown down, who accuses them day and night before our God" (12:10).

Satan's role in Revelation 12 of accusing Christians before God has roots in the earliest Old Testament references to him. In Job 1–2, Satan makes the accusation that the only reason Job is faithful to God is that God has been so good to him. Satan charges that if God were to allow him to suffer, he would curse God. So God gives Satan permission to test Job with suffering, to see how faithful to God he will remain.

In Zechariah Satan's role as accuser is even clearer: "Then he showed me Joshua the high priest standing before the angel of the LORD, and Satan standing at his right hand to accuse him" (Zechariah 3:1). The more common impression of Satan as tempter, rather than accuser, is clearer in 1 Chronicles 21:1: "Satan stood up against Israel, and incited David to number Israel" in a census (which God regarded and punished as sinful).

In Revelation 12 the blood of the Lamb and the witness of those willing to suffer for their faith conquer this accuser. This is good news for heaven, for if the accuser is not present when people appear before God in judgment, they will not be prosecuted. It is bad news for the earth and sea: "But woe to you, O earth and sea, for the devil has come down to you in great wrath, because he knows that his time is short!" (12:12). The end of this vision, when the dragon is angry with the woman and goes off to make war on the rest of her offspring, helps to explain the intensity of earthly persecution and suffering of Christians. This "bad news" is somewhat balanced by the hope that Satan is no longer in heaven waiting to ambush the faithful at God's judgment throne.

As symbol, this is powerfully consoling "good news-bad news." It explains not only Christ's victory over our accuser in heaven, through his death on our behalf, but also the sufferings Christians still endure from Satan here on earth. Recall, however, that symbols are not doctrine. For example, we cannot leap to the conclusion that if Satan the prosecutor has been expelled from the heavenly courtroom, then everyone will now avoid prosecution and therefore all humans will be saved. The rest of Revelation makes it clear that human resistance to God persists to the end and that hell awaits those who refuse to repent.

The Dragon and Political Beasts

At the beginning of the dragon's war against Christians, he stands on the sand of the sea (see Revelation 12:17b) and waits for the beast arising from the sea (see 13:1). John's visions indicate plainly that Satan attacks Christians primarily through human institutions and rulers. From the sea, which many at the time regarded as a fountainhead of chaos and of rebellion against God, comes the beast who, like the dragon (see 12:3), has ten horns with crowns and seven heads with blasphemous names.

To this beast who looks like him, the dragon gives all his power and authority (see 13:2). Therefore, some men worship both the dragon and the beast: "Who is like the beast, and who can fight against it?" (13:4). At the time of Revelation, most of the world was asking, "Who can fight against Rome?"

This beast emerging from the sea recalls the fourth and most terrible of the beasts from the sea in the vision in Daniel 7:1-8, a beast that also had ten horns (Daniel 7:7). Apocalyptic symbols can have different referents on different occasions. The fourth beast in Daniel originally referred to the Greek Empire under the legendary persecuting emperor Antiochus IV Epiphanes. By the time of Revelation, the symbol of the persecuting beast referred to the Roman Empire. For later readers it can refer to any "superpower" that seems especially hostile to Christianity or under the influence of Satan.

This beast was allowed to utter blasphemies, make war on Christians, and conquer them for the now conventional apocalyptic time span of forty-two months (see Revelation 11:2; the three and a half years of persecution first mentioned in Daniel 7:25; and the 1,260 days in Revelation 11:3, 12:6.) The equivalent numerical symbol in several visions of Revelation seems to refer to the period of persecution by the beast here in Revelation 13:5, to the subjection of Jerusalem by the nations in Revelation 11:2, to the time for the two witnesses to prophesy (see 11:3), and to the time for the woman to be protected in the desert (see 12:6, 14). All of these may well refer to the same "ideal" time of persecution, an intense but very brief time of dominance by Satan and his beasts and political and human instruments.

The Mark of the Second Beast
In Revelation 13:11 John has a vision of a second beast, this one coming out of the land. This beast has two horns like a

lamb—perhaps as a counterfeit imitation of and substitute for the Lamb. But though it looks like the Lamb, it sounds like the dragon.

Later in Revelation this second beast is usually referred to as a "false prophet" (Revelation 16:13; 19:20; 20:10) for two reasons. First, it tries to look like the Lamb and, thus, a good prophet, even though its voice and message is that of the satanic dragon. Second, its role is to lead people away from God. It works on behalf of the first beast and makes the earth worship it, and it meets that beast's ultimate fate in the lake of fire.

This second beast not only tries to look like the Lamb; it also mimics and counterfeits the marking on the foreheads of the 144,000 followers of the Lamb in Revelation 7:3. The beast "causes all, both small and great, both rich and poor, both free and slave, to be marked on the right hand or the forehead, so that no one can buy or sell unless he has the mark, that is, the name of the beast or the number of its name" (13:16-17). Whereas the mark or seal of the Lamb protects believers, the seal of the beast enables its followers to engage in economic activity, without which it is hard to survive in the secular world.

The persecution symbolized by this sealing is economic persecution of Christians, who could not be members of trade guilds or the like without submitting to the quasi-religious rites required for membership in those guilds. Nor could Christians engage in many forms of civil religion that were prerequisite for participation in the economic and political life in the Roman Empire and its provinces.

The seer challenges his readers to "break the code" of the number of the beast: "This calls for wisdom: let him who has understanding reckon the number of the beast, for it is a human number, its number is six hundred and sixty-six" (Revelation 13:18). Many scholars suggest that the original meaning of this code is the numerical numbers of the

Hebrew letters for Neron Kaisar, referring to Nero Caesar, the especially notorious emperor of Rome under whose violent persecution both Sts. Peter and Paul were martyred. Of course, the very nature of such mysterious codes is that they can be and were applied by Christian readers through the ages to later evil or persecuting rulers.

In contrast to this marking by the second beast, the 144,000 who have the Lamb's seal on their foreheads (see Revelation 14:1-5) now stand with the Lamb on Mount Zion (symbolizing the heavenly Jerusalem) and sing a new song before God's throne in heaven. These no longer have to be protected from punishment on earth, as they did in Revelation 7. The seer calls them the "first fruits" for God and the Lamb, gathered from the human race (14:4-5). This clearly implies both that they are now in heaven after being redeemed from their earthly perils and that they are the first among many who will be saved to live forever with God.

Visions of Wrath

Revelation 14 goes on to predict the fall of Babylon (see 14:8). One of many visions that portray God's judgment is that of the Son of Man on a white cloud (as in Daniel 7:13), ready to harvest the earth for God's wrath (see Revelation 14:14-20). Revelation 15 begins another series of visions, which also emphasize God's wrath. Throughout all of Scripture since Genesis, the problem of evil and injustice on earth has been crying out for a definitive remedy. In Revelation a major answer to the problem of evil is the wrath of God at the end of time, which finally brings justice to worldly situations in which injustice has been triumphant.

Again we see the common pattern in Revelation where John has multiple visions, which illuminate varying aspects of the same basic realities. Many visions and symbols in this section of Revelation represent God's punishment for the long history of human rebellion. "Then I saw another portent in heaven, great and wonderful, seven angels with seven plagues, which are the last, for with them the wrath of God is ended" (Revelation 15:1). Before reporting the seven plagues, John describes those who conquered the beast and its image and its number 666. They are singing a new version of the Song of Moses (see Revelation 15:3-4), which in Exodus 15 the Israelites sang after God saved them from Pharaoh at the Red Sea.

Further divine punishment is symbolized by the seven bowls of God's wrath given to the seven angels with the seven plagues (see Revelation 15:5–16:1). As these bowls are poured out, sufferings are inflicted on those who bear the mark of the beast, while the angel praises in song the justice of these divine judgments (see 16:2-7). As more sinners suffer from further bowls of wrath, they curse God but do not repent (see 16:8-11).

With the sixth bowl of God's wrath, the Euphrates River dries up, and foul demonic spirits like frogs come from the mouths of the dragon, the beast, and the false prophet. These summon kings of the whole world for a final battle against God at Armageddon (see 16:12-16). When the seventh angel pours out his bowl of wrath, a loud voice from the temple proclaims, "It is done!" There follow conventional apocalyptic signs such as lightning, earthquakes, and hailstones so great that the humans they fall on curse God for the plague (16:17-21).

When the seven bowls have been poured out, one of the angels addresses John: "Come, I will show you the judgment of the great harlot who is seated upon many waters" (Revelation 17:1b). The woman sits on a scarlet beast, which is full of blasphemous names and has seven heads and ten horns (illustrating the close relationship between the historical city of Rome and the beast, the symbol of the Roman Empire, see Revelation 17:3). This woman (Rome) has been called Babylon the great and is drunk with the blood of the saints and martyrs (see 17:5-6). In Daniel and earlier prophets, Babylon was already the symbol of a persecuting empire, based on its historical destruction of Jerusalem and of the first temple and on the exile of Judah.

In parody of the God "who is and who was and who is to come" (for example, in Revelation 1:4), the beast "was, and is not, and is to ascend from the bottomless pit and go to perdition" (Revelation 17:8, to be ultimately fulfilled in 20:1-3, 10). Another code for the symbols of the beast is announced in Revelation 17:9: "This calls for a mind with wisdom: the seven heads are seven mountains on which the woman is seated" (an obvious reference to the city of Rome built on seven hills).

The explanation of the code continues, interpreting the numbers of kings, of the beast, and finally of the ten horns as ten future kings who "are of one mind and give over their power and authority to the beast" (17:13). The horns or future kings will make war on the Lamb, and the Lamb will conquer them (see 17:14). In Revelation 17:15-18, the angel explains also how the horns and beast will eventually turn on the harlot and burn her. "And the woman that you saw is the great city which has dominion over the kings of the earth" (17:18), another obvious reference to the city of Rome.

Revelation 18 announces and exults in the fall of Babylon-Rome under God's judgment, including the mourning of merchants and sailors over their lost incomes. The city's wanton behavior and punishment are like those of the cities of Jerusalem and Samaria in Ezekiel 16. The ultimate and primary reason for God's judgment follows: "And in her was found the blood of prophets and of saints, and of all who have been slain on earth" (Revelation 18:24).

The Lamb Reigns

Revelation 19 begins with rejoicing in heaven over the judgment and punishment of Babylon-Rome.

> Hallelujah! Salvation and glory and power belong to our
> God, for his judgments are true and just; he has judged the
> great harlot who corrupted the earth with her fornication,
> and he has avenged on her the blood of his servants.
>
> REVELATION 19:1-2

The heavenly rejoicing increases in volume and focuses now on the reign of God and on the marriage of the Lamb to his Bride, who is clothed with the fine linen of the righteous deeds of Christians (see 19:5-8).

In the next vision John sees the "Faithful and True" rider on a white horse, who judges and makes war in justice (Revelation 19:11). The rider is the Word of God, who will smite the nations and rule them with a rod of iron (see Psalm 2:9). An angel then invites the scavenger birds to come for a great supper on the flesh of horses and men who are about to die in their fight against the rider and his army (Revelation 19:17-19), a powerful metaphor for the coming carnage among God's enemies.

The beast and false prophet are captured in this battle and thrown alive into the lake of fire, and the rest are slain by the rider and the sword from his mouth. "And all the birds were gorged with their flesh" (19:21). Many of God's enemies have been slaughtered and the two beasts thrown into hell. One last enemy remains: the dragon, Satan himself.

The Thousand-Year Reign

Perhaps the most perplexing passage in Revelation for Catholics and many other Christians is the vision of a thousand-year reign of Christ and Christian martyrs. A literalist interpretation of this passage is a key building block in many widespread contemporary notions of the rapture, tribulation, and related end time scenarios. Although some early patristic writers had similar millennialist interpretations, before long such interpretations were definitively and repeatedly rejected in official Catholic doctrine concerning the end times. How, then, are Catholics (and other Christians seeking alternatives to "left behind" rapture scenarios) to interpret this millennial reign?

First, a vision of the chaining of Satan for a thousand years grounds the possibility of the vision of a millennial reign that immediately follows:

> An angel...from heaven...seized the dragon, that ancient serpent, who is the Devil and Satan, and bound him for a thousand years, and threw him into the pit, and shut it and sealed it over him, that he should deceive the nations no more, till the thousand years were ended. After that he must be loosed for a little while.
>
> REVELATION 20:1-3

The seer repeats the explanation he gave in Revelation 12:9: The dragon of his visions is the same ancient serpent who in Genesis 3 precipitated the primeval sin and human rebellion against the Creator.

What this binding of Satan for a thousand years symbolizes depends largely on how one interprets the account of the thousand-year reign in Revelation 20:4-5:

> Then I saw thrones, and seated on them were those to whom judgment was committed. Also I saw the souls of those who had been beheaded for their testimony to Jesus and for the word of God, and who had not worshiped the beast or its image and had not received its mark on their foreheads or their hands. They came to life, and reigned with Christ a thousand years. The rest of the dead did not come to life until the thousand years were ended. This is the first resurrection.

This vision plainly portrays both Christ and the martyrs who died for him as the ones reigning on the thrones. These martyrs were mentioned earlier in Revelation. At the opening of the fifth seal John saw their souls under the altar, and they were crying out, "How long before thou wilt judge and avenge our blood on those who dwell upon the earth?" (Revelation 6:10). They were given a white robe and told to rest a little longer until the number of those to be killed as they were would be complete (see 6:11).

Although the vision does not specify whether these thrones are in heaven or on earth, all thrones of good authorities in the visions in Revelation have their location in heaven, which strongly implies that this too is a heavenly reign. Although the explanation at the end of the vision designates this living or coming to life as "the first resurrection" (Revelation 20:5), the customary verb for "being resurrected" is not actually used in verse 4, but simply "they lived [more literal than the RSV's 'came to life'] and reigned" with Christ one thousand years.

The vision also makes no reference to resurrected bodies of the martyrs but only to "the souls of those who had been beheaded" (Revelation 20:4). In Revelation 6:9 the same group were referred to as "the souls of those who had been slain." Despite the name given to what happens in this vision as "the first resurrection," the vision itself portrays only living souls of the martyred.

Focus on their souls alone does not imply a bodily resurrection but corresponds to what is most commonly held about life after death in the latest writings of the Old Testament and in the New. Mention of only their souls implies that those who continue to be alive after their death are in an intermediate state. They are living but bodiless souls before the ultimate general resurrection, when they will receive transformed, spiritualized bodies. This conforms to the point of view about afterlife in the rest of the New Testament, most explicitly in 1 Corinthians 15.

It is important to remember that the final sentence is still describing a vision, whose symbolic details are not to be spelled out in an overly literalist manner. If one interprets the final sentence, "The rest of the dead did not come to life [more literally 'did not live'] until the thousand years were ended" (Revelation 20:5) as a creedal or dogmatic statement rather than as the vision symbolism that it is, it would apparently clash with traditional creedal and Catholic dogma about the afterlife. The Creed summarizes much of Scripture when it implies (as the *Catechism* makes explicit) Catholic traditional beliefs. Immediately after dying, the immortal soul of the deceased faces its own private "particular judgment," preceding and distinguished from the public "general judgment" of all resurrected humans at the end of the world. After its particular judgment, the disembodied soul will live on in one of three possible states: in heavenly glory, in a temporary purifying preparation for heaven (purgatory), or in the eternal torments of hell (see *CCC*, #1051-1060). It will live thus until the general resurrection, when it will be reunited with its either glorified or "hellish" body to live out the consequences of its final judgment (see Matthew 25:32-33).

An Earthly Reign?
How, then, does one explain and interpret the vision in Revelation 20:4-6 of an intermediate thousand-year reign of Christ and the martyrs before the final judgment? An actual earthly reign before the final judgment of Christ at his *parousia* is utterly divergent from all the parables and sayings attributed to Jesus about the end times and from almost all of the end-time statements and scenarios in Pauline and other New Testament letters. Jewish expectations for the end times in the prophets and apocalyptic works can shed some light on why such an expectation was current in the first century.

There is virtual consensus that later apocalyptic end time writings tend to differ fundamentally from writings of the earlier prophets. These later writings give radically different solutions to the problems of evil and the expectations for divine intervention (with or without a royal [Davidic] Messiah). Prophetic writings tend to call readers to repentance and to social and political justice as ways to overcome evil (whether evil nations, persecutors, sinners, or sinful actions) in this world and within history. Parts of the Old Testament that were written earlier tend to struggle to explain the problem of evil within the limits of life on earth as we know it.

The later apocalyptic writings are much more pessimistic than the earlier prophets about the possibility of overcoming evil within history without a dramatic intervention of God. This intervention would essentially put an end to history by a final judgment, with rewards and punishments in the afterlife rather than within history during life on earth.

Thus, between earlier Jewish prophetic writings and the Jewish and Christian apocalyptic texts from about 200 B.C. to A.D. 200 (most of them not incorporated into our Bible), there were competing expectations and scenarios for the end times. The prophetic approach, which some rabbinical writings also perpetuated, looked forward to some kind of intermediate earthly reign of a Jewish Messiah or other savior figure for varying lengths of times, such as forty, four hundred, or one thousand years.[6] Apocalyptic writings, on the other hand, tended to despair of any perfectly just Jewish or other kingdom within history in this world. Apocalypses placed their hopes rather on God's bringing an end to history by judging and punishing sinners, oppressors, and persecutors of his people. Those writings that expected God to act through a Messiah (including Christian expectations for Jesus the Messiah) anticipated that the coming of the Messiah (for Christians, the *second* coming of the Messiah) would be associated with the end of the world and with a final judgment on the entire human race. This ultimate judgment would definitively divide humans into the just or saved in heaven and the unrepentant and damned in hell.

John reports visions that seem related to both kinds of concerns. In Revelation the undeniably primary expectation and scenario is an apocalyptic breaking in by God or Jesus to end history and to judge all humans, then reward or punish them. Yet the very different vision of the thousand-year reign here in Revelation 20 seems more closely related to a prophetic concern that there be some kind of vindication for those who suffered for their faith, however symbolically that might be described.

Some biblical exegetes who almost exclusively focus on historical criticism tend merely to mention without explanation both kinds of expectations as coexisting side by side in this book, without addressing the apparent contradiction between the millennial reign and the rest of Revelation and the New Testament. Other scholars make more effort to reconcile their historical critical results with concerns about the doctrines of their faith and church. They tend to interpret this dichotomy in at least two different directions.

Scriptural Evidence

One approach is to insist that "the tail must not wag the dog." It is hardly deniable that an expectation of a thousand-year earthly reign of the Messiah is virtually unique in the New Testament (a small minority of scholars also relate 1 Corinthians 15:22-28 to this perspective).[7] Almost all the New Testament passages dealing with the second coming of Jesus envisage only one return for ultimate judgment at the end of the world, without any earthly interregnum of a thousand years or of any other symbolic length of time.

Therefore, most church-oriented scholars refuse to interpret the vast majority of biblical passages based on one or at most two passages that might support a tiny marginal position. Other church-oriented scholars who believe in the rapture and dispensationalist interpretations do not hesitate to interpret the rest of the Bible according to this one passage and its (very) few possibly supporting passages.

My own instinct as both a believing Catholic and trained Scripture scholar is not to try to read too much into these verses nor to overinterpret them. My inclination is to recognize that they report a vision filled with symbolism rather than factual narration. This symbolism embodies and expresses a longstanding prophetic concern that there be at least some human vindication for upright and honest people who have suffered for their faith. It singles them out as having a special reign with Christ. However, even in this interpretation, the passage mentions only *souls* of the martyrs. It says nothing about being resurrected bodily but simply *living* to reign with Christ. Even in this interpretation, the reign of bodiless souls would have to be in heaven, not on earth.

Another important theological truth implicit in this symbolism of a thousand-year reign of the Messiah and his martyrs is that God is providing yet another opportunity for sinners to repent and return to God and his ways. Throughout biblical history, humans have experienced fluctuating circumstances regarding how severely they are tempted. Sometimes God's people lived under good kings who promoted obedience to God's covenant and commandments. At other times the people were acutely tempted by evil kings or by foreign oppressors toward apostasy. Often God then provided yet another opportunity for repentance.

In the end, however, God has always respected our freedom of choice between covenant fidelity to him and apostasy. That seems to be the theological point of this symbolic thousand-year period that is relatively free from Satanic temptations, followed in the end by a brief release of Satan for one final rebellion of Gog and Magog (that is, of all the hostile pagan nations) against God and his people. God's crushing of this last rebellion will be instantaneous and total:

> Fire came down from heaven and consumed them, and the devil who had deceived them was thrown into the lake of fire and sulphur where the beast and the false prophet were, and they will be tormented day and night for ever and ever.
>
> REVELATION 20:9b-10

The last enemy, the devil, will join the beast and false prophet forever in the lake of fire.

The Final Judgment

"Then I saw a great white throne and him who sat upon it" (Revelation 20:11). After his vision of God slaying the rebellious nations and casting the devil into the lake of fire and sulphur (hell), John sees God seated on the throne to judge all the resurrected dead. The symbolism for the universality of this resurrection for judgment is dramatic.

> And I saw the dead, great and small, standing before the throne, and books were opened. Also another book was opened, which is the book of life. And the dead were judged by what was written in the books, by what they had done.
>
> REVELATION 20:12

As Scripture repeats over and over, God is no respecter of persons: Great and small alike will have to stand before his throne to be judged by what they have or have not done.

The scene immediately preceding implies the destruction of the entire world and, therefore, the death of all humans: "From [God's] presence earth and sky fled away, and no place was found for them" (Revelation 20:11). Not only the dead who are in Hades (presumably because they were buried on dry land, according to ancient Greek mythological thought) but also the dead who lie unburied at the bottom of the sea are all resurrected to face judgment before God for their deeds (see 20:13). Finally the last enemies of God and humans, symbolized by death and Hades, are thrown into the lake of fire, "the second death" (20:14; see 1 Corinthians 15:26: "The last enemy to be destroyed is death"). Those humans whose unrepented evil deeds kept their names from being written in the book of life are also cast into hell (see Revelation 20:15).

Revelation 21 will narrate stirring visions of a "new heaven and a new earth" (21:1). But first the intense visions of Revelation 20 will demonstrate how all rebellion against the Creator will finally and definitively be crushed at the Last Judgment. The "destroyers of the earth" will be destroyed in hell.

The problem of evil will finally meet a thoroughly just solution: People who do unrepented evil deeds will be punished; the good will be rewarded. The injustices that the good suffer from evildoers in this life will be rectified in the next life. Total justice will be finally, and actually for the first time, publicly established. The bad news for evildoers is good news for the upright, who have been victimized and oppressed and persecuted by them in this life.

A New Heaven and a New Earth

"Then I saw a new heaven and a new earth; for the first heaven and the first earth had passed away, and the sea was no more" (Revelation 21:1). With the crushing of all evil, the old creation, which was perverted and undermined by human sin, no longer exists. Now God will provide a new creation that will restore the lost blessings of Eden. The sea, which in the old creation was an arena for and symbol of chaos and evil, the location from which originated the beast in Revelation 13, has no place in this new creation.

God's original plan for union with his human creatures

was rendered inoperative when humans rejected it. Now sin has been punished. God will ensure that his plan will, in fact, win out.

The New Jerusalem

> And I saw the holy city, new Jerusalem, coming down out of heaven from God, prepared as a bride adorned for her husband; and I heard a loud voice from the throne saying, "Behold, the dwelling of God is with men. He will dwell with them, and they shall be his people, and God himself will be with them; he will wipe away every tear from their eyes, and death shall be no more, neither shall there be mourning nor crying nor pain any more, for the former things have passed away."
>
> REVELATION 21:2-4

The new creation is not earthly but comes from above, from heaven. The Book of Revelation has no expectations or illusions that somehow we humans will be able to "build the kingdom of God on earth." The New Jerusalem is God's new creation, God's new Eden replacing the Paradise lost by human sin in Genesis.

The New Jerusalem is presented in personal terms, "as a bride adorned for her husband." This in the biblical worldview applies especially to the Church as the personal bride of Christ and mother of Christians (see Revelation 12:17). In the New Testament the Church is referred to as the body of Christ in two senses: Paul often describes the Church as the body joined to Christ the Head (as the branches are joined to Christ the Vine in John 15). The Church is also the body of Christ in the sense of the "one body" marital union with Christ in Ephesians 5.

Just as the earthly Jerusalem was a special locus of God's presence, especially in the temple located there, so the New Jerusalem is where God's dwelling is with humans. "Behold, the dwelling of God is with men. He will dwell with them, and they shall be his people, and God himself will be with them" (Revelation 21:3). God is already present in his Church before the end, but his presence will be experienced in the heavenly Jerusalem completely and without hindrance or limitation.

The result of God's dwelling with us intimately is his removal of all our pain and suffering: "He will wipe away every tear from their eyes, and death shall be no more, neither shall there be mourning nor crying nor pain any more, for the former things have passed away" (Revelation 21:4). Revelation provides the final answer to earthly suffering. After ridding creation of all evil and evildoers, God will personally heal and minister to his holy ones and free them from all their suffering. In the new Jerusalem God "will make all things new" (21:5).

> And he said to me, "It is done! I am the Alpha and the Omega, the beginning and the end. To the thirsty I will give from the fountain of the water of life without payment. He who conquers shall have this heritage, and I will be his God and he shall be my son. But as for the cowardly, the faithless, the polluted, as for murderers, fornicators, sorcerers, idolaters, and all liars, their lot shall be in the lake that burns with fire and sulphur, which is the second death."
>
> REVELATION 21:6-8

God's work of redemption through a new creation is now complete. God reaffirms his identity as origin and goal of all creation. Reiterating prophetic promises like Isaiah 55:1, God pledges to satisfy our human thirst for the infinite. God reassures those who have overcome sufferings and persecutions that their fidelity will result in the most intimate relationship with him: "He who conquers shall have this heritage, and I will be his God and he shall be my son" (Revelation 21:7).

On the other hand, God's perfect justice also demands that unrepentant sinners who have committed grievous sins will remain in perpetual alienation from God in the "lake that burns with fire and sulphur" (21:8). God completely respects our free human choices, whether to accept or to reject the love he offers. These human choices have enduring, even eternal, consequences.

Face-to-Face

The seer John then has another vision of the New Jerusalem, one much more descriptive of its appearance, measurements, and attributes than this first brief vision of Jerusalem. The holy city is coming down from heaven with God's glory and radiance. Its gates have the names of the twelve tribes inscribed, showing continuity with Israel, and on the foundations of the wall are the names of the twelve apostles of the Lamb (see Revelation 21:10-14). As in Ezekiel's vision, an angel measures the holy place, but in Revelation this is the city. The city is a huge and perfect cube, paralleling the perfect cube of the Holy of Holies in the temple from the time of Jesus.

In stark contrast to most Jewish visions of the New Jerusalem, including that in Ezekiel, this vision has no temple: "And I saw no temple in the city, for its temple is the Lord God the Almighty and the Lamb" (Revelation 21:22). In the earthly Jerusalem God's presence was concentrated in the temple; in the New Jerusalem God's presence extends throughout the entire city, making a temple unnecessary. Just as nothing unclean could enter the old temple, so nothing unclean can enter any part of the New Jerusalem. God's presence demands this.

Nor does the New Jerusalem have any sun or moon (which belong to the old creation), "for the glory of God is its light, and its lamp is the Lamb" (Revelation 21:23b). God's light will always shine in the New Jerusalem, so there will be no night, nor therefore will its gates ever be shut. The glory and honor of the nations will be brought into

Jerusalem, but no one unclean, "only those who are written in the Lamb's book of life" (21:27b). The New Jerusalem is a symbol of God's glory fully revealed to his people.

John in his visions sees also a river with the water of life (as in Ezekiel 47). But whereas Ezekiel's river flowed from the new temple, here the river flows "from the throne of God and of the Lamb," because the New Jerusalem has no temple (Revelation 22:1). Other aspects of the New Jerusalem also recall lost blessings from the garden of Eden. For example, the "tree of life" produces twelve kinds of fruits, one kind for each month, and the leaves of the tree are for the healing of the nations (a more universalistic view than comparable visions in Ezekiel 47).

There will not be anything accursed in the New Jerusalem, but "the throne of God and of the Lamb shall be in it, and his servants shall worship him; they shall see his face, and his name shall be on their foreheads" (Revelation 22:3-4, as in Ezekiel 9:4). Scripture generally considers this face-to-face vision of God to be impossible in this life, but biblical and Catholic faith alike look forward to this "beatific vision" of God in heaven. It will satisfy the infinite hunger within humans as nothing else ever could. This climactic vision repeats that the New Jerusalem will have no night, for God will be their light, and they shall reign forever and ever (see Revelation 22:5).

The epilogue to the vision emphasizes its trustworthiness. The words of the prophecy shall not be sealed up (as are apocalypses attributed to ancient seers like Enoch) "for the time is near" (Revelation 22:10b). Jesus repeats that he is coming soon (22:7, 12), that he will repay each person for what he has done, and that he is "the Alpha and the Omega, the first and the last, the beginning and the end" (22:13). The end of the Bible provides the seal for God's purpose, from the beginning of Genesis, for the creation of the world and for all humans within it.

Conclusion

The purpose of Revelation is, therefore, not to provide pieces of a biblical puzzle by which current or future generations (including generations in a future far beyond that imagined by the original writer and readers of Revelation) can construct and reconstruct blow-by-blow scenarios of God's termination of the present world and inauguration of his new creation. For centuries readers have been fruitlessly trying to do this. The result of their efforts is often a distraction from what the Bible is really trying to tell us about the end times.

God through Scripture is not laying down an exact account of how the world will end or how Satan will be defeated. The Bible is not a puzzle for the idly curious to construct into an end-time scenario. Nor does the Bible prematurely judge and separate the saved from the damned, the raptured from those left behind, in ways that can only lead to smugness about one's own group and prejudice against other groups of believers or nonbelievers.

Rather the Bible is trying to assure believers that God's original plan for creation will be reestablished conclusively when he sends his only Son a second time. Jesus will bring the world to complete justice, finalizing the salvation won by his death and resurrection. The first coming of Jesus has won the basic victory over sin and Satan: It has cast Satan from heaven (see Revelation 12). But the mop-up battles are not yet over. Satan continues to harass Christians through the persecutions of worldly and secular powers.

That harassment will be brought to an end, and God's justice will triumph completely over satanic forces, human sin, and rebellious disobedience. Jesus will return in glory as judge of the living and the dead. He will proclaim public vindication for those who love God and public sentence for unrepentant sinners, both satanic and human. Justice will at last be completely done, injustice will be terminated and punished, and oppressors will be definitively overcome.

The Bible explains the end times in terms of God's ultimate purpose of creation and in terms of his rescue of fallen humans through sending us his Son to be our Savior from sin, death, and Satan. It is a message of hope and warning and exhortation. From Genesis to Revelation, the Bible reveals the meaning of our lives, reconciliation through God's Son with our Creator God, the ultimate end of evil, hope for heavenly reward, and warning to avoid eternal punishment.

This is some of what I as a Catholic find when I search the Scriptures for what the Bible says about the end times. I pray that this reading will be helpful also to others.

Notes:

1. On the symbolic language of visions, see Norman Perrin and Dennis C. Duling, *The New Testament: Proclamation and Parenesis, Myth and History,* 2nd ed. (New York: Harcourt Brace Jovanovich, 1982), 120-23.

2. Augustine, *Confessions,* 1.1.

3. Charles H. Talbert, *The Apocalypse: A Reading of the Revelation of John* (Louisville, Ky.: Westminster John Knox, 1994), 113.

4. David E. Aune, "Revelation 1-5" in *Word Biblical Commentary,* 52a (Dallas: Word, 1997), 90-91.

5. See Talbert, 35.

6. Talbert, 93-94.

7. Raymond F. Collins, *First Corinthians,* Sacra Pagina Series, Vol. 7 (Collegeville, Minn.: Liturgical, 1999), 552, discusses but rejects the interpretation of an intermediate reign in 1 Corinthians.

Index

Abraham
    choosing of, 85–86
    story of, 2
Acts of the Apostles, 47, 103
Adam
    God's image and, 19
    indwelling sin and, 119
    Jesus as, 115–116
    reversal of, 111–114
    in Romans, 114–116
afterlife
    Catholic belief in, 170
    in New Testament, 169
Antiochus IV Epiphanes, 68, 70, 75
    death of, 76
    persecution by, 77–78
    as "son of perdition," 133
Apocalypse
    Revelation and, 137
apocalypses, 2
    creation and, 137
    evil and, 4
    Jesus' message of, 83–110
    symbols for, 153, 162
    writings of, 67–68, 95–96, 139,
        143, 148, 171
apostles, 125–126

Babylon
    condemnation of, 48
    fall of, 164
    judgment, punishment to,
        166–167
baptism, 107
beast
    code for, 165–166
    as "false prophet," 163
    Revelation and, 161–162
    second, 162–164
Bible. *See also* New Testament; Old
Testament; specific Books
    catastrophes and, 96–98
    code language in, 95–96

creation and, 180
end times and, 2, 73–74, 180–181
evil and, 4, 141
God's image, likeness in, 18–20
God's purpose and, 179
numbers in, 73–75
origins and, 7
symbolism in, 72, 73
theological plot of, 141
"Book of Consolation," 42
Book of Daniel. *See also* Daniel
    apocalyptic visions in, 69–71
    apocalyptic writing and, 67–68
    Babylon in, 166
    King Nebuchadnezzer's dream
        and, 68–69
    martyrs, resurrection in, 77–80
    "one like a son of a man" vision
        in, 71–73
    time calculations in, 73–77
Book of Ezekiel. *See also* Ezekiel
    "dry bones" prophecy of, 60–61
    God's chariot throne in, 50–52
    God's transcendence and, 50
    Gog of Magog in, 61–62
    Lord's glory leaving temple in,
        54–56
    oracle of comfort in, 58–59
    pagan pretensions in, 56–57
    restored temple, land in, 62–65
    sacred river in, 65–67
    shepherds' condemnation in,
        57–58
    vision of watchman in, 53–54
    visions of, 50–67
Book of Isaiah. *See also* Isaiah
    "Book of Consolation" in, 42–43
    Chapters 40-55 in, 37–39
    God as Creator in, 9
    God's judgment, mercy and,
        32–33
    "Isaiah Apocalypse" in, 35–37
    Mount Zion and, 43